# Ancient Mysteries and Modern Masonry

# Ancient Mysteries and Modern Masonry

Charles H Vail

# CONTENTS

ADULTBRAIN
publishing

# INTRODUCTION

The purpose of these lectures is to consider the origin and nature of the Ancient Mysteries and Modern Masonry and to show the relation which they bear one to the other. Freemasonry deals largely with the morals and symbols of the Mysteries of Antiquity, and originally was one of the channels of Ancient Wisdom.

There were a few among the founders of Modern Masonry who possessed the Royal Secret, or, at least, had a knowledge of its existence, and, if the key has been lost, the Mason, as Heir-apparent of the Old Wisdom, should be foremost in the search for its recovery.

All agree that the Masonic symbols and traditions are of the greatest antiquity, and can be traced to the far East--to the earliest civilization, from which time and place they have spoken in nature's language to all peoples of the earth. We are more and more convinced that this picture language of our ritual contains a most complete philosophy--a knowledge embracing the eternal verities of the universe, and that these symbols were designed by the Initiates of old to preserve and convey that Ancient Wisdom to the present and future generations. Though empires and dynastic continents have appeared and passed away, these ancient symbols, hewn in rock-cut temples and monuments, have served to convey the Great Secret from ages past and will continue its record as long as this part of the universe remains.

Modern, Masonry, has become in a special sense, the custodian of these ancient symbols; and should not be content with its possession only, nor with merely imitating its various predecessors; but should enter boldly into the inheritance of its birthright and seek the Ancient Wisdom of its illustrious prototypes. To confine the interpretation of its symbols and legends to lessons in morality and fraternity, such as are found in all exoteric religions, is not to grasp the deeper meaning that the glyphs and parables were meant to convey. Many to-day realize this fact and they are seeking still "More Light"--without, as well as within the tiled doors of our Lodges.

In setting forth the results of modern research concerning the symbols and legends of antiquity and their meaning in Modern Masonry, I shall not lift the veil from the secrets of the Order, but will endeavour to lead the initiate to the clearer light that he may not only see for himself the connection, linking the past with the present; but will begin to know, through

the development of his higher Masonic manhood, the mighty truth of which these symbols speak. In this endeavour I shall only refer to those things in Masonry that are exoteric and contained in our best publications. I do not claim the knowledge that would enable me to completely unfold the mystery and philosophy embodied in the glyphs of ancient times, but that they do embody an occult science no thinking man of to-day has any doubt, and if I am able to throw even a little light on the great subject of ancient symbolic mysteries I shall feel amply repaid for my efforts.

I am sure the lectures will prove interesting and instructive to both members and non-members of the Order, and while some few things mentioned will be better understood by Master Masons, my meaning will be clear to all: and that they may lead to a better understanding of the Ancient Mysteries and Modern Masonry, I bespeak for the subject matter your careful

# LECTURE I

THE ORIGIN AND OBJECT OF THE ANCIENT MYSTERIES.

Along with the popular traditions and public cults of ancient times, there existed an inner organization of religion--the Mystery Institution--which was the channel of secret traditions.

While our knowledge of the Mysteries is not so extensive as we could desire, owing to the fact that they were anciently guarded with the greatest care -- the slightest violation of the oath of secrecy being punishable by death--we know that the mystery-side of religion, a knowledge of its highest cult and doctrines, was only attained through initiation. Every great Teacher of antiquity passed through these portals. This one fact in itself makes the study of the Mysteries of the utmost importance to Masons.

The Institution of the Mysteries was to be found in all parts of the world. There were the Mysteries of Isis and Osiris in Egypt, the Mithraic Mysteries of the Persians, the Orphic and Bacchic and the later Eleusinian semi-Mysteries of Greece, the Mysteries of Samothrace and Chaldea, the Mysteries of India, the Druidical Mysteries, the Gothic Mysteries, and many others.

Thus it follows that the key to antiquity is a knowledge of its Mysteries. The late Gen. Albert Pike, formerly Sovereign Grand Commander of the Supreme Council, Southern Jurisdiction, A.A.S.R. illustrates this by saying: "Through the veil of all the hieratic and mystic allegories of the ancient dogmas, under the seal of all the sacred writings, in the ruins of Nineveh or Thebes, on the worn stones of the ancient temples, and on the blackened face of the sphinx of Assyria or Egypt, in the monstrous or marvellous pictures which the sacred pages of the Vedas translate for the believers of India, in the strange emblems of our old books of Alchemy, in the ceremonies of reception practiced by all the mysterious Societies, we find traces of a doctrine everywhere the same, and everywhere carefully concealed. The occult philosophy seems to have been the nurse or godmother of all religions, the secret lever of all the intellectual forces, the key of all divine obscurities, and the Absolute Queen of Society, in the ages when it was exclusively reserved for the education of the Priests and Kings." (Morals and Dogma, p. 729.)

THE ORIGIN OF THE MYSTERIES.

The Mysteries had their origin in the first great Teachers and Guides of humanity. These are called the "Sons of Venus," they formed the! "Nursery of Adepts"-- the nucleus of the first Great White Lodge. The Chief of these is known by many mystic names in the old writings--the "Root Base of the Occult Hierarchy," the "Kumara," etc. Surrounding the Chief there was a small band of Beings who came to earth to labour for the evolution of young humanity. Another class of Beings who aided in this work was called Agnishvattas. Many of these, we are told in the "Stanzas of Dzyan," became Arhats. Thus was established upon earth, according to tradition, the first Great Occult Hierarchy.

In the early ages occult knowledge was taught openly, as the sciences are taught in our colleges to-day. But in the course of time many allowed their selfishness to rule and so abused their power that it became necessary to withhold such knowledge from the unworthy. This was the condition of religious affairs when the Mysteries were necessarily established by the King-Priests of the Divine Dynasties, in the days of Atlantis.

There were many already in possession of occult knowledge who were so engrossed in selfishness that they could not be brought into the divine path; and their abuse of this power over the forces of nature made them giants of evil. They rebelled against the White Emperor, and became Black Magicians, this caused a long and fierce struggle. At last the cup of evil was full; the forces of nature were turned against the land, until the great continent, together with all followers of their own selfish practice, sank beneath the waters of the ocean. Before the storm broke, however, the men of the "Good Law" heeding the summons to escape, migrated to a place of safety.

Before the overthrow of Atlantis the Mysteries were well established in ancient Chaldea and Egypt --the two great Fourth race nations being offshoots of the great Atlantean civilization. The Indian Mysteries came from her own Priest King, the Manu, who gave to the first branch of the Aryan stock its religious teaching. From this fount of the Aryan race the Mystery-teaching in after years flowed westward, and mingling with the older tradition, derived from Ancient Atlantis, gave to, it new life and power. The Greeks received their Mysteries from Orpheus, who introduced them direct from India. But from whatever source the various nations received their mystic instruction, the meaning was ever the same--all Initiates were members of the one Great Brotherhood. In these early days the

Mystery-Institutions were conducted by Great Adepts

whose knowledge was the fruitage of a prior system of evolution; but as time went on and our humanity developed, the great Masters gradually withdrew, and the Mysteries were committed to the advanced pupils of our present system of evolution.

THE SOURCE OF RELIGIONS.

There are two schools of thought in the modern world-- Comparative Mythologists and Comparative Religionists. The answers given by these two schools to the question of the source of religion are diametrically opposed, but both base their arguments upon the same common facts. These facts are of marked similarity, not only in the teaching, character, and power of the Founders of religions, but also of the main outlines of their lives.

The stories of these Saviour-Gods and their teachings antedate, some of them by many centuries, the birth of the Christian Saviour. This similarity amounting in many cases to practical identity, denotes, according to both schools, a common origin.

The Comparative Mythologists contend that the common origin is one of common ignorance, that the universal natural phenomena and the personification of these powers of nature, resulted in similar ideas. This school maintains that the loftiest religious sentiments and doctrines are merely the refined feeling and expression of the barbarous guesses of primitive men; that Animalism, Fetishism and Nature-worship are the soil out of which the highest forms of religious flowers have blossomed and that the founders of the great religions are the highly developed but lineal descendants of the "whirling medicine man."

On the other hand, the Comparative Religionists maintain that the common origin is one of Divine Wisdom, or Gnosis. All religions, they say, originate from the teachings of Divine Men, who constitute a

great Brotherhood of Spiritual Teachers, and give out from time to time, to different races and nations of the world, such parts of the fundamental truths of religion as are suited to the needs of the people.

They contend that Animalism, Fetishism, and Nature-worship are the distorted and dwarfed

descendants of true religious belief, and that the founders of great religions are men who have advanced beyond normal humanity, thus becoming the spiritual guardians of the race.

We have no hesitancy in saying that we accept the view of the Comparative Religionists, for the Scriptures of the various religions furnish abundant evidence that the founders were advanced men, and their teachings are not surpassed (or often equalled) by later writers in the same religions. The Sacred Books of the East give ample evidence of this fact; while the alleged refining process of the Mythologists is without adequate support.

We also find among savages many traces of lofty ideas which are entirely beyond their capacity to originate. When we remember that the savage tribes of to-day are not our ancestral types, but rather the degenerate off-spring of past great nations, we begin to understand how they came to possess these lofty ideas--they are the faint remaining vestiges of the Wisdom long ago imparted by a great religious Teacher.- (Esoteric Christianity, Besant, Ch. I.)

It is evident that man in his infancy was not left to grow up unaided. There have always been Elders or Sages from whom the less advanced brethren received direction and training; such ever stood beside the earliest cradle of humanity, and gave to the race the needed guidance and impulse toward a higher ideal of civilization.

The first great Teachers were advanced souls from other and still earlier systems of evolution. They were the Adepts of the early races who established upon this earth the first great Occult Fraternity. These lofty Beings watched over and guided early mankind; and as men advanced and became fitted for higher knowledge they were instructed in the nature of the gods, the human soul, the mysteries of the unseen world, and the processes of the world's continual evolution. Such-are the persistent and uncontradictory facts in connection with the Mysteries.

Religions, then, have their source in the Occult Hierarchy--the qualified guardians of the spiritual growth of the human family.

REASONS FOR ESOTERICISM.

History has noted the disastrous results of spreading occult knowledge indiscriminately, and since the sad experiences of Atlantis, the Initiates have carefully guarded from the unpurified that knowledge which is power. Therefore, the most rigid conditions regarding purity, unselfishness and self-control are imposed on all who seek the higher knowledge. The temptation to use power for selfish ends is too great to entrust such knowledge to men of uncontrolled desires.

Another reason for esotericism is the fact that religions were given for the purpose of quickening human evolution. Men are at such various stages of development, that what will be understood by the philosopher is unintelligible to another, and in order to reach and help all, it is evident that instruction must be adapted to the peculiar needs of each individual. The religious teachings must be as graded as evolution itself--each must be met on their own level and helped on and on, from that plain to greater heights and broader views, all in a fashion that appeals to their unfolding intellects. It is due to this fact that all the great Teachers have reserved the greater truths for those capable of receiving and understanding them.

SECRECY OF INITIATES.

This has been the method of all great instructors. Initiates of all ages have maintained a profound silence concerning the truths learned in the Mysteries. From Orpheus, the first Initiate, of whom history catches a glimpse, to Pythagoras, Confucius, Buddha, Apollonius, Jesus, Saccus, no Teacher ever committed anything to writing for indiscriminate public use.

Herodotus, in speaking of the reasons why animals were worshipped, says: "If I were to explain these reasons, I should be led to the disclosure of these holy matters, which I particularly wish to avoid," and again in other matters, "Concerning these, at the same time that I confess myself sufficiently informed, I feel myself compelled to be silent. Of the ceremonies also in honour of Ceres, I may not venture to speak, further than the obligations of religion will allow me."

Jesus charged his disciples that they tell no man that he was the Christ, also saying, "Give not that which is holy unto the dogs, neither cast ye your pearls before swine; lest they trample them under their feet and turn again and rend you." He surely had good reason for his secrecy. Many have learned the wisdom of these words when too late; Anaxagoras, Pythagoras, and Socrates, are notable examples.

The great Teachers instructed their chosen disciples in

the higher knowledge and propagated these truths in allegories and parables. "All that can be said concerning the Gods," says Strabo, "must be by exposition of old opinions and fables; it being the custom of the ancients to wrap up in images and allegory their thoughts and discoveries concerning nature."

Pythagoras, the great mathematical Mason, divided his classes into the exoteric and esoteric, and his secrets were forbidden to be committed to writing.

The Society of the Essenes, among whom were St. John the Baptist and St. John the Evangelist, made similar distinctions; dividing their adherents into Neophytes, Brethren, and Perfect, while Ammonius Saccus obliged his disciples by oath not to divulge his doctrines, except to those who had been thoroughly instructed and prepared.

In Egypt we find the same method in practice, for Clement says, "The Egyptians did not entrust the mysteries they possessed to all and sundry, and did not divulge the knowledge of divine things to the profane." He also informs us that the sphinxes erected in front of the temples and places of Initiation denoted silence and secrecy--that all sacred truth is enfolded in symbolical fables and allegories--and he says of the Mysteries, "Those who instituted the Mysteries, being philosophers, buried their doctrines in myths, so as not to be obvious to all." . (The Stromata, Book V, Ch. VII, Ch. IX.)

The Sages of Greece, according to Pausanias, "Never wrote otherwise than in an enigmatical manner." They concealed their knowledge under the veil of fiction and so taught that the vulgar might not comprehend. The typical Hermes assembled his disciples in a holy place or shrine where strict secrecy was imposed. In the Perfect Sermon he says, "And ye, O Tat, Asclepius and Ammon, in silence hide the mysteries divine within the secret places of your hearts, and breathe no word of their concealment." This was the universal procedure.

Says Wm. R. Singleton, 33d degree, Past Grand Secretary, Grand Lodge of the District of Columbia: "The wisdom of the Chaldeans, Phoenicians, Egyptians, Jews of Zoroaster, Sanconiathon, Pherecydes, Syrus, Pythagoras, Socrates, Plato; of all the ancients, that is come to our hand, is symbolic. ... . In the method explaining the various symbols, religion and philosophy were veiled in allegoric representations ... These symbols were displayed openly in the temples ... to the profane altogether obscure, but streaming with beams of light to the Initiated." (History of Freemasonry and Concordant Orders, p. 83.)

## OCCULT SYSTEMS OF WRITING.

There were various methods employed by the teachers to convey and yet conceal the truths of the Mysteries. The three main Kabbalistic systems are the Gematria, which is based on the numerical value of words-- applying to the letters of a word the sense they bear as numbers; the Temura, by which a word yields its mystery by anagram --the transposition of the letters--and the Notaricon, which may be compared to stenography. The system of number-letters was derived from Chaldea by the Hebrews during and subsequent to their captivity.
The Chaldeans worked out their cosmogonies and
anthropogeneses in numbers, their sacred books were written with this object in view; Pythagoras had a number-philosophy, which in all probability held many resemblances to the numberbooks of Chaldea; this method was developed to a great extent by the Hellenising tendencies of the cultured Rabbis of Alexandria. The Gnostics also made much use of this number-symbolism-- the system of Marcus being quite elaborate, and the books of Hermes are probably the oldest repositories of number-symbolism in western civilization.

Closely connected with this was Geometrical symbolism, which was also used by Pythagoras-- the square, triangle, point within the circle, cube, double triangle, 47th. problem of Euclid, etc., the geometrical figures representing the numbers objectively. In every cosmology from the earliest times we find the basic idea combining numerical geometrical figures.

There is also the allegorical method--a setting forth of truth in the form of myths, or parables, and furthermore, the secret sacerdotal tongue, the Senzar, which was known to the Initiates of every nation. Then to rightly read the world's Scriptures one must have the keys to all these various systems.

OBJECT OF THE MYSTERIES.

The object of the Mysteries was the instruction and development of man. They were the work of genius employing the sciences and a profound knowledge of the human heart in the task of purifying the soul, and seeking man's felicity by the means of virtue. Great emphasis was laid upon man's immortality, and the object and purpose of the Mysteries was to fit him for a blessed state beyond. Thus these mysteries taught the condition of the postmortem state, and strove to develop in the candidate the powers that would enable him to verify the instruction for himself.

Antiquity had held that there was a science of the soul, a knowledge of things unseen, a Gnosis; and now that the possibility of extending the bounds of

consciousness beyond the physical plane has been proven by many experiments in psychism, the claim of the Mysteries is not beyond rational belief. That the ego may transcend the limits of the body and become conscious on the higher planes of nature verifies the truth of the mysteries of all ages and proves that nature's God, in infinite wisdom, through the constant progress or development of his children, is initiating them from every field of labour to aid in his mighty work.

The higher instruction was not only given by perfected Initiates who could function on the higher planes, but the assistance of angelic hierarchies was also invoked and those exalted Beings came to teach and elevate by their presence. Iamblichus, the great Theurgist of the third and fourth centuries A.D. says, "The Gods [these Beings are not Gods in the Western sense of the term but Angels, or Devas; Plato calls them the 'Minor Gods' to distinguish them from the Supreme] "being benevolent and propitious, impart their light to Theurgists in unvarying abundance, calling up ward their souls to themselves, procuring for them a union with themselves, and accustoming them, while they are yet in body, to be separate from bodies, and to be led around to their eternal and intelligible principle." For "the soul having a twofold life, one being in conjunction with body but the other being separate from all body," it is most necessary to learn to separate from the body, that thus it may unite with the Gods and learn the truths of the intelligible world. (Esoteric Christianity, p. 24, 25.)

The consummation of all this was to make the Initiate a God, either by union with a Divine Being without or by the realization of the Divine Self within.

Sallust says that the object of the ceremonies of Initiation was to unite man with the world and Deity. The Initiate claimed that the soul purified from all stain, could see the Gods in this life-- that is, could attain the beatific vision, and hold communion with the Immortals. Prof. Harnick remarks that deification was the idea of salvation taught in the Mysteries.

The Greek Neo-platonists called, this state "Theophany," which means either communication between the Gods or God and those Initiated mortals who are spiritually fit to enjoy such intercourse; or the presence of a God in man, an incarnation or blending of the personal Deity; the Higher self with the lower

self--its representative on earth.

Plotinus defines this state as "The liberation of the mind from its finite consciousness, becoming one and identified with the Infinite." The length and frequency of this sublime condition depends upon the spiritual

development. Proclus claims to have experienced this ecstasy six times during his mystic life; Plotinus states that he had reached this state "but three times as yet ;" Porphyry asserts that Appolonius attained this state four times, while he experienced it but once, and that after he was sixty years of age. This illumination may come and go as a flash, or it may last for hours. With the high Initiates, the Word is really made flesh, the union complete, and its duration continuous throughout life. The Mysteries were as a training school to this end. Philo in speaking of the Divine Vision says, "It is the special gift of those who dedicate themselves to the service of

That-which-is.... to ascend by means of their rational faculties to the height of the aether, setting before themselves 'Moses'--the Race that is the friend of God (The Race of the Logos) as the leader of the way ... . the work of philosophy is naught else than the striving clearly to see these things."

Proclus also says, "In all the Initiations and Mysteries, the Gods exhibit many forms of themselves, and appear in a variety of shapes; and sometimes, indeed a formless light of themselves is held forth to the view; sometimes this light is according to a human form and sometimes it proceeds into a different shape." (Quoted in Eleusinian and Bacchic Mysteries, Taylor, p. 66.)


Taylor too, correctly infers, "The most sublime part of the epopteia or final revealing, consisted in beholding the Gods [high planetary spirits] themselves, invested with a resplendent light." (Ibid, or same book, p. 65.)

In Plato's Phaedo, Socrates is made to say, "Those who instituted the Mysteries for us appear to have been by no means contemptible, but in reality to have intimated long since that whoever shall arrive in Hades unexpiated and uninitiated shall lie in mud [a symbol of the gloomy surroundings of the lowest region of the astral world], but he that arrives there purified and Initiated, shall dwell with the gods." (Plato, Cary's Translation, Vol. I, p. 68.) Again in Phaedrus, Plato says, "Initiated into that which may be rightly called the most blessed of all Mysteries. which we celebrated when we were whole and unaffected by the evils that awaited us in time to come, and moreover when we were initiated in, and beheld in the pure light, perfect, simple, calm, and blessed visions, being ourselves pure, and as yet unmasked with this which we now carry about with us and call the body, fettered to it like an oyster to its shell." (Ibid, p. 326.)

If we admit the existence of faculties in man capable of piercing the veil of matter, we shall find no reason for rejecting the plain evidence of ancient writers

that the Mysteries were associated with a psychic and spiritual revelation.

Hermes in his sermons has much to say on the Gnosis. Gnosis of God is the science of sciences. In "The Key" he tells us that "The distinctive feature of Good (God) is that it should be known." This is the "Vision Glorious." As stated by Mead in his commentary, "This consummation of Ecstasis (the extension of consciousness), we are told, was a transcending of the limitations of body, and was a faculty possessed by the forbears of the 'race' into which Hermes and now Tat are being born." ( Thrice Greatest Hermes, Vol. II, p. 162.) The nature of Ecstasy is further explained as the fruit of meditation and contemplation. "The Gnosis of the Good is holy silence and a giving holiday to every sense." This is in accord with the Yoga of the Upanishads, which shows identity of thought of those who have had first hand experience. Hermes proceeds, "For it is possible, my son, that a man's soul should be made like to God, e'en while it still is in a body, if it doth contemplate the Beauty of the Good." This is the true deification or apotheosis--Man is like God in that he becomes a God. The result of the evolution of the soul was the attainment unto the "first steps of deathlessness," spoken of by Paul as the "resurrection of the dead." "The soul's vice," says Hermes, "is ignorance . . . . But on the other hand, the virtue of the soul is Gnosis. For he who knows, he good and pious is, and still while on the earth divine." Here we have the attainment of the divine state, that of Adeptship while still in the body.

Proclus held that Initiation elevated the soul, from a material, sensual, and purely human life, to a communion and celestial intercourse with the Gods; and that a variety of things, forms, and species were shown to Initiates, representing the first generation of the Gods.
In speaking of Petosiris, Proclus tells us that this Egyptian Philosopher had an intimate knowledge of every order of the Gods and Angels, and refers to a hieratic formula of theurgic invocation to the greatest of the

goddesses (Necessity), for inducing the vision of this power. Valens tells us of Nechepso who attained to direct knowledge of the Inner Way. Vettius, in the first half of the first century A. D. laments that he did not live in those days of Initiate Kings, Rulers and Sages who occupied themselves with the Sacred Science. In those days so great was their love for the holy mysteries, so high their virtue, that they left the earth below them, and in their deathless souls became "heaven walkers" and knowers of things divine.

Vettius also quotes a Greek apocalyptic treatise of

Nechepso where the king tells us that he had remained in contemplation all night gazing into the aether; and

so in ecstasy he left his body and had then heard a heavenly Voice addressing him. This Voice was not merely a sound, but appeared as a substantial presence, who guided Nechepso on his way through the heavenly space. (Thrice Greatest Hermes, Vol. I, p. 101.)

Cicero considered the establishment of the Eleusinian Mysteries to be the greatest of all benefits conferred by Athens on other commonwealths; their effect having been to civilize men, soften savage ferocious manners, and teach them the true principles of morality, which initiate man into the only kind of life worthy of him. (Cicero cited in Morals and Dogma, p. 380.) The Mysteries procured for man a real felicity on earth by means of virtue. He was taught the immortality of the soul and the inflexible laws of divine justice, and the great moral precepts were made known not only to the Initiates but also to the profane. The Mysteries pointed out to men the way to "live better and die happier;" but, as we have seen, the object of the Mysteries was not merely to teach morality, for as Gen. Pike well says, "Had moral truths alone been taught the Initiates, the Mysteries could never have deserved nor received the magnificent eulogiums of the most enlightened men of Antiquity--of Pindar, Plutarch, Isocrates, Diodorus, Plato, Euripides, Socrates, Aristophanes, Cicero, Epictetus, Marcus Aurelius, and others: philosophers hostile to the Sacredotal Spirit, or historians devoted to the investigation of Truth.

No: all the sciences were taught there; and those oral
or written traditions briefly communicated, which reached back to the
first age of the world." (Ibid, p 373.)

The object of the Mysteries, then, was to instruct men in the real science
of being, and to lead them up the stairway to perfection--to the super-
human stage--to the Christ and that which transcends even perfect Mas-
terhood.

In this way they sought to purify the soul, holding that the true home
of the soul was in the higher spheres, the earth a place of exile, and that
to return to its birthplace the soul must free itself from the power of the
world--must be emancipated from the passions and the hindrances of
the senses. The Mysteries taught men how to attain the dominion of the
soul, which was absolutely necessary as "We must flee from everything
sensual," says Porphyry, "that the soul may with ease reunite itself with
God."

Thus the Mysteries sought to sanctify men, to illuminate their souls and
fit them to return consciously to union with the Deity. The Gnostics
all claimed that a man could so perfect himself that he would become
a conscious worker with the Logos. The object of the Mysteries, then,
was not only to teach

the unity of God and the immortality of the soul, as Warburton,
Mackey and other Masonic writers contend, but to enable each man to
verify these great spiritual facts for himself.

These citations from the ancient classic writers and philosophers regarding the Mysteries might be greatly extended, but this will suffice to show
the reverence and admiration in which the Mysteries were held. Would
these Mysteries have received such high praise had they not known them
to be of divine origin? As has been well said, "When men like Pythagoras, Plato, and Iamblichus, renowned for their severe morality, took
part in the Mysteries and spoke of them with veneration it ill behooves
our modern critics to judge them upon their merely external aspects."

Many have accepted without question certain derogatory statements of the early Christian Apologists concerning the Mysteries, without taking into consideration the fact that the writers were animated by the spirit of bitter controversy. Due allowance should be made for this, placing such statements in the same category as those of the Pagans, when they charge the Christians with being Atheists, and practicing shameful rites. To suppose that the Mysteries were the invention of charlatanism is the height of absurdity. True, they degenerated in the lapse of time as did the Christian Agape but in the beginning and for long ages they were pure and noble, and the wisest and best men of antiquity were not wiIful falsifiers.

The Mysteries were truIy the greatest institutions of ancient times. They contained all that was most profound in philosophy and most spiritual in religion.

Such were the Ancient Mysteries of which Masonry is the successor.

## LECTURE II

THE EGYPTIAN, HINDU, AND PERSIAN MYSTERIES.

Undoubtedly the ceremonies of Initiation were originally few, and all were intended to symbolize the progress of the human soul--they were the outward signs of an inward fact. Initiation, as we shall see in a subsequent lecture, was regeneration--a real spiritual "new becoming" or re-birth. The candidate himself became the thing symbolized--Hermes, Buddha, Christ, etc. This state was the result of real Initiation--an evolution of the human into the divine.

In the course of time this spiritual truth was neglected and initiation no longer meant spiritual regeneration, and the rites no longer typified the various stages of the soul's progress -   the mystic

birth, death, and resurrection. The key to the spiritual science was forgotten,--the Master's Word "lost,"-- and Initiation consisted mereiy in imparting to the candidate the traditional knowledge of the symbols as handed down from time immemorial, and gradually the true meaning of the symbols disappeared, and even the symbols themselves were transformed into crude dogmas.

THE CEREMONIES OF INITIATION.

The Ancient Mysteries were divided into two stages -- the Probationary Path and the Advanced or Path Proper. In most schools the Probationary Path was merely preliminary, but, as some schools began with the preliminary in numbering the stages or divisions, one needs be on guard to avoid misunderstandings. Others, as in Greece, divided their Mysteries into the Lesser and the Greater. Beyond which there was the True Mystery of the Path. (In other systems the True and the Greater Mysteries were undoubtedly the same.)

The higher evolution belonged to the True or Real Mysteries, to which all others led. A Neophyte was compelled to be proficient along these lines before he was allowed to take the real Initiation and enter upon the Path proper, which will be considered in a subsequent lecture. There were outer forms and ceremonies which stood for and symbolized the True Mysteries, but little was known of their inner nature except by those who experienced them.

The ceremonies were undoubtedly altered in the course of time, but even in the days of the greatest deterioration we find traces of the hidden wisdom in connection with the ancient symbols--some of which have survived, and are to be found in Modern Masonry.

TEE EGYPTIAN MYSTERIES.

The learned Greek Plutarch, himself an Initiate into the Osireaca, of which there was probably a thiasos at Delphi, gives much valuable information regarding the Mysteries of Egypt. Of course, he could only give hints, for, as he says, in speaking of the Priests, "Their philosophy--which for the most part was hidden in myths and words (logoi) containing dim reflections and transparencies of truth, as, doubtless, they themselves make indirectly plain by fitly setting sphynxes up before the temples, as though their reasoning about the Gods possessed a wisdom wrapped in riddle. . . So great, then, was the care Egyptians took about the wisdom which concerned the mysteries of the Gods. And the most wise of the Greeks also are witnesses--Solon, Thales, Plato, Eudoxus, Pythagoras, and as some say, Lycurgus as well--through coming to Egypt and associating with ker priests," and "brought

back to the memory of his men their symbolic and mysterious [art], containing their dogmas in dark sayings.... When, therefore, thou hearest the

myth-sayings of the Egyptians concerning the Gods-- wanderings and dismemberings, and many such passions-- thou shouldst remember what has been said above and think none of these things spoken as they [really] are in state and action." (Plutarch: Concerning the Mysteries of Isis and Osiris, Sec. IX, X, XI.) This is true not only of the Egyptian myths but of all others.

Plutarch then sets forth the Osiris and Isis

Mystery-Myth. It begins with the birth of the Gods-- Osiris, the Elder Horus, Typhon, Isis, etc. Osiris and Isis being in love with each other were united. They ruled over Egypt for many years but finally the malicious Typhon, his evil brother, while filled with envy sought his destruction. He devised a beautiful chest, and having it brought into the banquet hall, promised to give it to any one whom it would exactly fit. Osiris stepped in and laid down, whereupon they who were present rushed up and put on the lid and fastened it down, and carried the chest to the river Nile, whence it was borne out on the flood to the sea. When Isis heard what had been done she set forth in search of the chest, which, meanwhile, had been carried by the waves to the Byblos country, where the land-wash brought it to rest in a certain heather bush or tamarisk tree, a species of acacia. This bush grew around, enfolded and hid it entirely within itself. The King Malkander marvelled at the greatness of the tree, and cut it down and made of it a prop in the form of a pillar for his roof, but Isis having found trace of the chest and its disposition through Anubis and the daemonean spirit of a voice, came also to Byblos and sitting down by a fountain head showed attention to the maids of the Queen, dressing their hair with ambrosia, thus securing an invitation to the palace, where she became nurse of the Queen's little child; then finding time ripe to reveal herself, the Goddess claimed

for-her own the pillar of the roof, and taking it down,

she cut the tree from around the coffin and placing the chest in a boat, carried the body to her son Horus, who concealed it in a deep forest. But Typhon while out hunting came upon it, and recognizing the body as that of Osiris, tore it into fourteen parts, and scattered them abroad. Isis, hearing what had been done, sought to recover the parts, and succeeded in finding all but one, which had been cast into the river and eaten by the fishes. Horus then fought Typhon and overpowered him, when it was proclaimed that Osiris had risen from the dead.

This is merely an outline of the myth. It has a macrocosmic and microcosmic meaning. In the former sense, Osiris and Isis are cosmic or super-cosmic beings, symbolized by the sun and moon, and the elder

and younger Horus are the Intelligible and Sensible Worlds. Microcosmically the Myth pertains to the mystery of Initiation--the Horus or Christ stage of manhood. In this latter aspect it symbolizes the mystic life of the Initiate.

In regard to Initiation Plutarch says, "When the Initiates of Isis at their 'death' are adorned in these [robes], it is a symbol that this Reason (Logos), is with them; and with Him and naught else they go there [or walk there, that is, in Hades,--the death here mentioned is the mystic death unto sin]. For it is not the growing beard and wearing cloak that makes philosophers, O Klea, not clothing in linen and shaving oneself that makes Initiates of Isis; but a true Isiac is one who, when he by law receives them searches out by reason (Logos) the [Mysteries] shown and done concerning these Gods and meditates upon the truth in them." (Ibid, Sec. III.)

This Mystery rite is referred to by Epiphanius as solemnized in the Temple of Isis who is called the Virgin Mother, or World Virgin. In speaking of the Feast of Epiphany, which was a great day in Egypt connected with the birth of the Aeon (a phase of the birth of Horus) he says, "Indeed, the leaders of the idol-cults, filled with wiles to deceive the idol worshippers who believe in them, in many places keep highest festival on this same night of Epiphany (the manifestation of Light), so that they whose hopes are in error may not seek the truth. For instance, at Alexandria, in the Koreion, as it is called an immense temple--that is to say, the precinct of the virgin; after they have kept all night vigil with song and music, chanting to their idol, when the vigil is over at cock-crow, they descend with lights into an underground crypt, and carry up a wooden image lying naked on a litter, with the seal of a cross made in gold on its forehead, and on either hand two similar seals, and on both knees two others, all five seals being similarly made in gold. And they carry around the image itself, circumambulating seven times the innermost temple, to the accompaniment of pipes, tabors, and hymns, and with merry-making, they carry it down again underground. And if they are asked the meaning of this mystery, they answer and say: 'Today at this hour the Maiden (Kore), that is, the Virgin, gave birth to the Aeon.' In the city of Petra also, the same is done, and they sing the praises of the Virgin .... and him who is born from her, Dusares, that is, Alone Begotten of the Lord. This also takes place in the city of Elousa on the same night just as at Petra and at Alexandria."

Epiphanius as an outsider could not be expected to understand the rites he describes, and as a narrow bigot he could not be expected to deal with them

fairly. But the importance of the passage is the testimony it bears to the fact that one of the most widespread mystic festivals was connected with a "rite of resurrection." You notice here the "crowing of the cock" which is connected with the crucifixion of Jesus, and the cross marked on the forehead, hands, and knees or feet of the image, or the one who has returned from the Underworld (Hades).

Epiphanius tells us that the mystic rite represents a macrocosmic mystery. Very true, but it also represents a microcosmic mystery. The mystic birth, death, and resurrection, were familiar to all the schools and corrLmunities of ancient times, and the mystic "rising again from the dead" was an integral part of the universal mystic-drama.

The Initiations of Egypt are described by C. W. Lead-beater, a well known theosophical writer, as follows: "The candidate was attired in a white-robe, emblematic of the purity which was expected, and brought before a conclave of priest-initiates in a sort of vault or cavern. He was first formally tested as to the development of the clair-

voyant faculty which he had been previously instructed how to awaken, and for this purpose had to read an inscription upan a brazen shield, of which the blank side was presented to his physical vision. Later he was left alone to keep a kind of vigil. Certain mantrams, or words of power, had been taught him, which were supposed to be appropriate to control a certain class of entities.   Other
ceremonies of the Egyptian Mysteries are of interest. .
. . At one stage of his advancement the candidate laid himself upon a curiously hollowed wooden cross and, after certain ceremonies, was en-tranced. His body was then carried down into the vaults underneath the temple or pyramid, while he himself 'descended into Hades,' or the un-derworld-- that is to say, in our modern nomenclature, he passed on to the astral plane. Here he had many experiences, part of his work being to 'preach to the spirits in prison;' for he remained in that trance condition three days and three nights, which typified the three rounds and the in-ternals between them, during which man was going through the earlier part of his evolution, and descending into matter. Then after 'three days and three nights in the heart of the earth,' on the morning of the fourth day, 'he rose again from the dead,' that is . . . . his body was brought back from the vault, and so placed that the rays of the rising sun fell upon his face and he awoke. This symbolizes the awakening of man in the fourth round, and the commencement of his ascent out of matter on the up-ward arc of evolution." (Some Glimpses of Occultism, p. 73 )

According to Pietschmann, the Egyptian Mysteries had

three grades, called Mortals, Intelligences, and Creators of Light. The Mortals were probationary pupils, who were instructed in the doctrine, but who had not yet realized the inner vision: The Intelligences were those who had attained the inner vision and had become men and re-ceived Mind. The Creators or Sons of Light were those who had be-come one with the Light--had attained to true spiritual consciousness. These three stages are called by W. Marsham Adams, Initiation, Illumination and Perfection. This state could be attained while yet in the body, and included the after death consciousness as a part of its content.

The ancient temples of Initiation in Egypt were models of the "Heavenly Jerusalem," a type of the
world-building, to use a Jewish Gnostic term. Adams describes the temple at Denderah thus, "In the center of the temple is the Hall of the Altar, with entrances opening east and west; and beyond it lies the great hall of the temple entitled the Hall of the Child in his Cradle, from whence access is obtained to the secret and sealed shrine entered once a year by the high priest, on the night of midsummer." (The Book of the Master, or the Egyptian Doctrine of the Light Born to the Virgin Mother, Adams, p. 24.) There were also various other halls and chambers, such as Hall of the Golden Rays, Chamber of Gold, Chamber of Birth, Dwelling of the Golden One, Chamber of Flames, all having reference to the Mysteries of Light and a divine Birth. "The chief Hall of the temple was the Hall of the Child in his Cradle, and the chief representation on the planisphere is the holy Mother with the divine Child in her arms." (Ibid, 24.)
THE HINDU MYSTERIES.

**************

The Mysteries of India were celebrated in temples carved out of solid rock; and in pyramids and dark pagodas. The temple of Elephanta is perhaps the most ancient in the world. It is one hundred and thirty-five feet square and eighteen feet high, supported by four massive pillars, and its walls are covered with statutes and carved emblematical decorations. The temples of Salsette exceed in magnitude those of Elephanta, though they are excavated in rock, their external form being pyramidal. The interior has many galleries and secret caverns, and in the inmost recesses of the structure a "cubical cista"--a sepulchre where the candidate was laid during his entranced state.
An account of the Initiation is given by Dr. Oliver in his History of Initiations which we herewith condense as follows:
The mysteries were divided into four degrees. The

candidate might perform his first probation at the early age of eight years. This consisted of an investiture of the Zennar or sacred cord of three threads, corresponding to our "cable-tow." This investiture was attended with numerous ceremonies and ended with an extended lecture from the preceptor.

After this the candidate was clothed in a linen garment without searns, and a cord put over his right ear, and he was placed under the care of a Brahmin, as a spiritual guide, to be instructed in the necessary qualifications for the Second Degree. He was subjected to many hardships and rigid penances and was taught to preserve the purity of his body, to avoid external defilements and to devote much time to study of the sacred books. At the age of twenty, if he were found to have made suitable proficiency in the preceding degree, he was admitted on probation to the Second. Here his austerities were doubled. At the conclusion of this probation he was Initiated into the privileges of the Mysteries. Sanctified by the sign of the Cross, which wals marked on every part of the body, he was subjected to the probation of Pastos, which was denominated the door of Patala or hell--the Tartarus of the Grecian Mysteries. This was the Mystical death. His perfection of the probationary period being attained, he was led, at the dead of night, to the cave which had been duly prepared for his reception; the interior of this cavern blazed with a light equal to the meridian sun. There sat in rich and costly robes the three chief hierophants, stationed in the East, West and South to represent the Sacred Triad--Brahma, Vishnu, and Siva, with the attendant Mystagogues, clad in holy vestments seated around. The well known signal from the sacred bell summoned the aspirant into the center of the august assembly; when the ceremony commenced with an anthem and solemn invocation. The oath was then administered, after which the candidate was sprinkled with water, and a mantra pronounced. He was then divested of his shoes, that the consecrated ground on which he stood might not be polluted, and was then made to circumambulate the temple three times, exclaiming each time on his arrival in the south, "I copy the example of the Sun, and follow his benevolent course." Here we have the origin of the preparation of the candidate, the circuits, etc., of Modern Masonry.

At the conclusion of the circuits, the candidate was placed in the care of a spiritual guide, and directed to observe proper silence during the succeeding ceremonies. He was then passed through seven ranges of dark and gloomy caverns; amid the din of howls, shrieks and dismal lamentations, a sudden explosion was heard which seemed to rend the mountains; flashes of light strearned before his eyes, and then all was darkness and silence. Gradually he beheld shadows and phantoms of various shapes, some with many hands, arms and legs, while others had none; the rnost terrible and frightful

figures appeared, all typifying the generation of the Gods, and other sacred mysteries.

The candidate then personified Vishnu, and was made to perform his numerous Avatars. In the fifth manifestation he took three steps at right angles, from which we get the three steps, as in the Master's degree, ending at right-angles. A]l these experiences were designed to teach certain lessons, and illustrate important truths, as the seven caverns, for instance, bore an allusion to the seven-fold division of the invisible world--the seven places of reward and punishment.

After all these trials, the pealing Conch was sounded, the folding doors were thrown open, and the candidate was conducted into Paradise, which was a spacious apartment blazing with a thousand brilliant lights, ornamented with statues and emblematical figures, decorated profusely with gems and jewels. With eyes riveted on the altar, he was taught to expect the descent of the Deity in the bright pyramidal fire that blazed upon it. This gorgeous display filled the mind of the aspirant with admiration, and lighted up theholy fervor of devotion in his heart. And now being fully regenerated, a new name was given him, expressive of his recently attained purity, and he was introduced to the chief Brahmin, in the midst of the august assembly, who received him as a brother and associate, invested him with a white robe and tiara, seated him in an elevated place, and solemnly delivered the signs, tokens, and lectures of the Order. His forehead was marked with a cross. An inverted level or tau cross, was inscribed on his breast, this was a badge of innocence and a symbol of eternal life. He was invested with the sacred sash or belt, and finally, he was entrusted with the sublime Name which was known only to the Initiated. The Arch Brahmin then entered on an explanation of the various emblems which were arranged around him; with the arcana of the hidden science enfolded under the holy gloom of the mysterious veil.

'An extensive system of symbolical instruction was also used in the Hindu Mysteries, and their philosophy was veiled under the impervious shade of hieroglyphical symbols, unintelligible to the profane, and intended to lead them into a maze of error, from which it was difficult to extract a single idea which bore any semblance to the original truth. These symbols were publicly displayed in their temples, bearing streams of light to the Initiated; while to the profane they were but an obscure mass of unintelligible darkness. (Oliver's History of Initiations, Ch. II.)
THE PERSIAN MYSTERIES.
The Persian Mysteries or the Mysteries of Mithras are

among the most important of antiquity. Even Pythagoras is said to have travelled from Greece to receive Initiation at the hands of those Persian Hierophants. The candidates were prepared for Initiation by various lustrations and forty degree-days of probation, which ended by a fifty-days fast. These trials were undergone in a subterranean cavern, where the candidate was bound to perpetual silence. At the conclusion of his probation he was guided into the Hall of Initiation, and received on the point of a sword presented to his naked left breast. He was conducted into the inner Chamber where he was purified by fire and water, and then conducted through the seven stages of Initiation. Dr. Oliver describes these stages as follows: "From the precipice where he stood, he beheld a deep and dangerous vault into which a single false step might precipitate him down to the 'throne of dreadful necessity,' which was an emblem of those infernal regions through which he was about to pass.

Threading the circuitous mazes of the gloomy cavern, he was soon awakened from his trance of thought, by seeing the sacred fire, at intervals, flash through its recesses to illuminate his path; sometimes bursting from beneath his feet; sometimes descending on his head in a broad sheet of white and shadowy flame. Amidst the admiration thus inspired, his terror was excited by the distant yelling of ravenous beasts; the roaring of lions, the howling of wolves, the fierce and threatening bark of dogs. Enveloped in blackest darkness, he was at a loss where to turn for safety; but was impelled rapidly forward by his attendant, who maintained an unbroken silence, towards the quarter from whence the appalling sounds proceeded; and at the sudden opening of a door he found himself in a den of wild beasts, dimly enlightened with a single lamp. His conductor exhorted him to courage, and he was immediately attacked, amidst the most tremendous uproar, by the initiated, in the forms of lions, tigers, wolves, grifflns, and other monstrous beasts; fierce dogs appeared to rise from the earth, and with dreadful howlings endeavored to overwhelm the aspirant with alarm; and how bravely so ever his courage might sustain him in this unequal conflict, he seldom escaped unhurt.

Being hurried through this cavern into another, he was once more shrouded in darkness. A dead silence succeeded, and he was obliged to proceed with deliberate step, meditating on the danger he had just escaped, and smarting under the wounds he had received. His attention, however, was soon roused from these reflections and directed to other dangers which appeared to threaten.- An undefined rumbling noise was heard in a distant range of caverns, which became louder and louder as he advanced, until the pealing thunder seemed to rend the solid roclcs and burst the

caverns around him; and the vivid and continued flashes of lightning, in streaming sheets of fire, rendered visible the flitting shades of avenging genii, who, frowning displeasure, appeared to threaten with summary destruction these daring intruders into the privacy of their hallowed abodes. Scenes like these were multiplied with increasing horror, until nature could no longer endure the trial; and when the aspirant was ready to sink under the effects of exhaustion and mental agony, he was conveyed into another apartment to recruit his strength. Here, a vivid illumination was suddenly introduced, and his outraged feelings were soothed by the sound of melodious music, and the flavor of grateful perfumes. Seated at rest in this apartment, his guide explained the elements of those invaluable secrets which were more fully developed when his initiation was complete.

Having pronounced himself disposed to proceed through the remaining ceremonies, a signal was given by his conductor, and three priests immediately made their appearance; one of whom, after a long and solemn pause, cas~ a living serpent into his bosom as a token of regeneration; and a private door being opened, there issued forth such howlings and cries of lamentation and despair, as struck him with new and indescribable emotions of terror. He turned his eyes with an involuntary motion to the place from whence these bewailings appeared to proceed, and beheld in every appalling form, the torments of the wicked in Hades.

Turning from this scene of woe, he was passed through some other dark caverns and passages; until, having sucessfully threaded the labyrinth, consisting of six spacious vaults, connected by winding galleries, each opening with a narrow stone portal, the scene of some perilous adventure; and having, by the exercise of fortitude and perseverance, been triumphantly borne through this accumulated mass of difficulty and danger; the doors of the seventh vault, or Sacellum, were thrown open, and his darkness was changed into light.

He was admitted into the spacious and lofty cavern already described, which was denominated the sacred grotto of Elysium. This consecrated place was brillinatly illuminated, and sparkled with gold and precious stones. A splendid sun and starry system emitted their dazzling radiance, and moved in order to the symphonies of heavenly music. Here sat the Archimagus in the East, elevated on a throne of burnished gold, crowned with a rich diadem decorated with myrtle boughs, and habited in a flowing tunic of a bright cerulean tincture; round him were arranged in solemn order the Presules, and dispensers of the mysteries; forming altogether a reverend assembly, which covered the awe-struck aspirant with a profound feeling of veneration; and by an involuntary impulse, frequently produced an act of worship. Here he was received with congratulations; and after having entered

into the usual engagements for keeping secret the sacred rites of Mithras, the sacred words were entrusted to him, of which the ineffiable Tetractys, or Name of God, was the chief. (History of Initiation, Oliver, Ch. IV.)

The candidate was then instructed in the secret science. The meaning of the emblems was explained, the incidents experienced converted to a moral purpose, and their significance made clear. Nothing was done without a purpose and every experience illustrated some truth and fact in nature. What they were designed to set forth we shall see in subsequent lectures.

Suffice it here to say, that the Mithra-Mystery was identical with the Christ-Mystery--the mystery of man's perfection and final apotheosis.

"The secret of regeneration, of being born anew or spiritually, or from above in brief, the di~inizing of man, was the last word of the Mithra-rites; all else is introductory or ancillary. This secret was the one secret of all the great mystery-rites and mystery arts." (Mysteries of Mithra, Mead, p. 47.)

A Ritual dealing with the mystery of apotheosis and used by the most advanced in the Mithraic esoteric circles has recently been discovered. It is a

"yoga-rite," one far in advance of the lower grades of Initiation. Initiation does not mean consummation--it is merely starting things going The candidate, to make the initiation valid, must "seal up the links," so to speak, and this Mithraic Ritual has to do with the final stages of spiritual evolution. (For complete exposition of this Ritual see "A Mithraic Ritual," by

G. R. S. Mead.)

Besides the various rites of Initiation already described, we find the same sacraments in the Mysteries that in later years were administered in the Christian Church Justin Martyr, 150 A. D., says that the evil demons in the Mysteries of Mithras aped the Christian Eucharist, for there was an offering of bread and of a cup of water with certain explanatory sacred formulae. (Justin Martyr First ~pology, Vol. II., Sec. LIV, LXII, LXVI, Second Apology Sec. XIII.)

Tertullian, 210 A. D., in speaking of the Mithraic Mysteries, says, "He, too, baptizes some--that is, his own believers and faithful followers; he promises the putting away of sins by a laver (of his own); and if my memory still serves me, Mithra there, (in the kingdom of Satan,) sets his marks on the foreheads of his soldiers; celebrates also the oblation of bread, and introduces an image of a resurrection, and before a sword wreaths a crown." (Prescription against Heretics, Ch. XL.)

Tertullian also explains the identities by resorting to the convenient theory of the Devil aping the Christian forms. But this curious explanation will hardly find adherents to-day--it is difficult to accept the earlier as copies, and the more recent as originals. We shall see later the origin and meaning of these similarities. Thus we find in the ancient Egyptian, Hindu and Persian Mysteries, a system of religious culture and training that originated thousands of years ago, and which through many centuries preserved and handed down the Master's Word to those who had made sufficient progress, and were thereby "duly and truly prepared" to receive it.

These great Institutions were the wonder of the world, hence it is not strange that they received the highest praise from all the great men of antiquity.

# LECTURE III

THE DRUIDICAL, GOTHIC, GRECIAN, AND JEWISH MYSTERIES.

We are to continue in this lecture our examination of the Mysteries of antiquity. We will consider first

THE DRUIDICAL MYSTERIES.

The Druidical Mysteries were the same as the Celtic, and were celebrated in many countries. We are told by Caesar that these Mysteries were better understood in Britain than anywhere else.

All temples, in whatever country, had places of Initiation connected with them, and they were usually subterranean. The great grotto at Castleton in Derbyshire bears evidence that the celebration of the Druidical Mysteries was of an elaborate nature; the temple at Abury was also a stupendous structure. and was built in the form of a circle.

The periods of Initiation were quarterly and were held at the time of the equinoxes and solstices. There were three degrees in the Druidical Mysteries-- Eubatesl, Bards, and Druids, and it was obligatory that the candidate for Initiation be well qualified and duly prepared--mental and moral perfection being the first requisite. When the candidate had passed the probationary stage he was clad in a robe, striped with white, blue, and green, emblematical of light, truth, and hope, and confined in a cromlech (tomb) for parts of three days without food,--dead, in the language of the Mysteries,--after which he was liberated for Initiation, and restored to life on the third day. This confinement preceded his Initiation into each of the two first degrees. When the Aspirant was liberated he

was placed in the hands of an officer and conducted around the sanctuary nine times, at first with slow and measured step, which at length was increased to a rapid pace. During the circuits there was a clang of musical instruments and recitations in praise of those who were heroic in war, courteous in peace, and the friends of religion. At the completion of this ceremony the oath of secrecy was adrninistered and the aspirant then went through various ceremonies in which he represented many characters, declaring among other things, "I have died," and "I have revived," alluding to his mystical death and resurrection.

In the second part of the ceremony there was the dismal darkness, the direful shrieks, the barking dogs, etc., with which we have been made familiar in the preceding Mysteries. The aspirant finally emerged from the gloom, and found himself surrounded with the most brilliant coru~cations of light, being then presented to the Archdruid, who instructed him in the Mysteries, imparting the knowledge of Druidism, and exhorting him to the practice of virtue.

There was still another degree to be administered to those who aspired to a high degree of perfection. To obtain this further advancement they were subjected to the most arduous purification and were committed to the tomb for nine months, where in solitude they studied theology, philosophy, cosmogony, astronomy, etc. Dr.
Oliver says this was "The death and burial of the Mysteries; and on its expiration he was said to be newly born from the womb of Ceridwen, and was pronounced a regenerate person, cleansed from his former impurities by the mystical contents of her cauldron." (History of Initiation, Oliver, p. 146.)
When the period of gestation in the womb of Ceridwen was complete, as the confinement in the tomb was termed, the candidate was ready for further instruction. Another trial, however, must be braved before the highest degree of light could be conferred. The candidate, now called the "new born infant," was placed in a boat, and committed to the mercy

of the waves. If he succeeded in securing a safe landing place, he was triumphantly received, and this completion of the Three Degrees made the aspirant, a "thrice born"--conferring upon him the power of inspiration and prophecy in the highest form.

The Druids maintained a high intellectual standard, for they taught their disciples astronomy, botany, anatomy, languages, medicine, etc. Thus we see the Mysteries were always repositories of Wisdom.

THE GOTHIC MYSTERIES.

The Gothic Mysteries were practiced at one time by all

the northern nations of Europe; we trace their introduction to Sigge, a Scythian Prince, who lived in the first century B. C.

There were three great festivals connected with the Gothic Mysteries. The most significant was celebrated at the winter Solstice and dedicated to Thor. The next celebration was dedicated to Frea and commenced at the second moon in the new year. The third was dedicated to Odin and was held in the spring. These were the principal celebrations, but Initiations were also performed at many smaller festivals held during the year.

The Palace of Thor, the principal place of Initiations, contained five hundred and forty halls and was situated in the kingdom of Thurdwanger.

The Gothic Mysteries, like all others, were connected with the Mystery Myth, differing only in detail. The Gothic version runs as follows: Balder, who was esteemed as invulnerable, had in the general assembly placed himself in sport as a mark at which the gods exercised their skill in casting darts. Odin and Friga exacted an oath of safety in favor of Balder from everything in nature except the mistletoe, which was omitted on account of its weakness. Loki discovered the exception and placed a sprig in the hands of the blind Hoder, persuaded him to cast it at Balder, who fell, pierced through with mortal wounds. His body was then placed in a boat and set afloat on the water, while the gods mourned for his decease. "The fable of Balder and Loki," says Dr. Oliver, "with the lamentations of the gods for the death of Balder, bears such an obvious relation to those of Osiris and Typhon, Bacchus and the Titans, Cama, Iswara, etc., that I entertain no doubt but that it constituted the Legend of Initiation; as it is, indeed, the exact counterpart of all other systems of mysterious celebration." (Ibid, p. 174, note 34.)

It would be needless repetition to go into detail regarding these Initiations. Suffice it to say that after the candidate was duly prepared, by the usual fasting and the preliminary ceremonies of sacrifice, processions, etc., he was conducted with naked feet into the sacred hall and through a winding pathway, amid shades of darkness and the howling of dogs, to the tomb of the prophetess Volva. Here occured the mysterious rites of invocation. Passing onward the candidate hears the bewailings for the death of the God, Balder. He was then confined in the Pastos or tomb, and guarded by Heimdal, the door keeper of the Gods; upon liberation he was instructed to search for the body of Balder, and to endeavor to raise him from death to life.

Before starting on his dangerous expedition he was

recommended to the protection of the Gods. The guide then conducted him through nine subterranean passages, where various experiments of awe and terror awaited him. Completing his journey he entered the illuminated sacellum, and found Balder enthroned on a seat of highest distinction. His entrance was greeted with an anthem of congratulation, and great rejoicing took place for the resuscitation of the God. The candidate then took a solemn oath on a naked sword--a symbol of the supreme God. Throughout the ceremonies the candidate had been impersonating Balder--that is, his experiences were the same as Balder's, who, as a perfect Initiate, is the type or first fruits of human evolution. The candidate had then attained the

Balder-state of manhood.

## THE GRECIAN MYSTERIES.

The Mysteries were introduced into Greece by Orpheus. This great Teacher evidently led one of the waves of emigration of the Aryan stock into Europe. The Orphic tradition had various fortunes. In the days of Homer it was neglected, for the people were too proud to listen to what they regarded as the superstition of their forefathers, but with the rise of philosophy in the seventh century B.C. the earlier religious Myths were again examined, and it became evident that ancient Greece poslsessed a Mystery-tradition which compared favorably with that of other nations. We do not know exactly the time when the Mystery institutions were established but we do know that they existed under various names-- Eleusinian, Bacchic, Dionysiac, Samothracean, etc., and that all were practically the same. The Eleusinian were perhaps the most noted as they constituted what might be called the State Mysteries. In these there were two divisions--the Lesser and the Greater, beyond which was the true Mystery of the Path. The center of the work of the Lesser Myster- ies was at Agrae; the Greater at Eleusis. The Lesser Mysteries dealt prin- cipally with Hades or the Astral world; the Greater with the Mental or Heavenly world. The ceremonial garment in the Lesser Mysteries was a fawn skin; in the Greater Mysteries a golden-fleece, The candidates for Initiation were naturally divided into two classes--those who were only capable of re-ceiving instruction in the things pertaining to the unseen, and those who were capable of special training in the development of clairvoyance; instruction was aIso given in cosmology, anthropogenesis, etc.

The Eleusinian Mysteries were celebrated with much pomp and lasted nine days. The places of Initiation, like those of other nations, were great subterranean caverns, containing many chambers and sepulchres in which the candidate was immured during a part of the

ceremonial rite. Some of these places of Initiation, with their tombs cut into the solid rock, are described at length by Mr. Maundrill. Every tem- ple had a cavern connected with it for Initiation. In some countries the place of Initiation was a pyramid erected over a subterranean cavern.

The first portion of the ceremony among the Greeks was the purifica- tion by water. The candidate was then conducted to the vestibule and invested with the sacred robes, and after being exhorted to courage the aspirant was led through a series of caverns, where he met with practically the same experiences as we have found in the other Mysteries--the dark and gloomy surroundings, the pealing thunder, the howling dogs and wild beasts, the flashes of vivid light, monstrous appearances, etc. After three days of these terrors, he was confined in a cell for reflection. Dr. Oliver says, "This was the symbolical death of the Mysteries; and the deliverance from confinement was the act of regeneration or new birth; and hence the rejuvenated aspirant was termed twice born; once from the womb of his natural mother and again from the pastos of Initiation." (Ibid, p.

98.) This deliverance was rather a resurrection than a new birth; the latter applying more properly to the first stage of Initiation, although, in one sense, every stage that marks an extension of consciousness is a new birth.

While the aspirant was undergoing the mystical death of Bacchus, the Initiates acted out the Myth. We have seen that this passion-vision was a part of every

mystery-drama. The neophyte here experienced the Great Passion himself. This feeling was a prerequisite to knowing. What it was we do not know, but it had to do with the mystic death of the Master. During this part of the drama there were loud lamentations over the death of their God, and Rhea, like Isis, went in search of his remains.

At a given signal from the Hierophant the mourning was turned into joy, for it was announced that the body had been found and restored to life. The candidate was liberated from his confinement, and after various experiences in the infernal regions, gained the verdant plains of Elysium, where the souls of the just were observed in the enjoyment of pure delights.

Here the Hierophant delivered a lecture on the purpose of the Mysteries; gave the usual instruction in the secret science, and bestowed the insignia of the Order. Clement says of the Greek Mysteries, "After these (the lustrations) are the minor Mysteries, which have some foundation of instruction and of preliminary preparation for what is to come after; and the great Mysteries, in which nothing remains to be learned of the universe, but only to contemplate and comprehend

nature and things," (Stromata, Book V, Ch. XI.)

The Bacchic or Dionysiac Mysteries grew to be mere festivities toward the last, and Bacchus himself regarded as the god of wine, instead of the manifestation of the Logos. The Mysteries of Greece and Rome shared the same decadence as the nations. We cannot Judge them by their relics, any more than we can judge the grandeur of Rome by the period of her decay.

Besides the public Mysteries there were the ancient schools of philosophy of Pythaagoras and Plato, which have sometimes been called the private or philosophic Mysteries. The founders of these schools were Initiates. Pythagoras is said to have been initiated into the Egyptian, Chaldean, Orphic and Eleusinian Mysteries. These schools of philosophy worked in connection with the Mystery-teaching. It is a mistake to suppose that Pythagoras and Plato formulated a new doctrine, for their philosophy was part and parcel of the old Wisdom which had been handed down by the Hierophants through the Mysteries. The genius of these great teachers consisted in clothing the great truths, enshrined in the ancient Myths, in modes of thought suitable to the time. In the Pythagorean schools the students were divided into three degrees or classes.

The followers of Pythagoras were noted for purity of life and loftiness of aim and purpose, and the higher religious life of Greece is to be sought in this connection.

There were also Orphic communities which deserve mention. The members of these communities were known as Orphics, and were said to live the Orphic life,--a life of holiness. It was with these communities that the Pythagareans took refuge when their school at Crotona was broken up.

THE JEWISH MYSTERIES.

The ancient Jews had their Mysteries, as well as all other peoples of antiquity. Mr. Elbe in his book (Future Life, p. 107) says that it appears to be an estaslished fact that the Israelites had their Mysteries, as well as the Egyptians and the majority of ancient races. Although they had these secrets, occult knowledge and kabbalistic teaching,--which passed form mouth to ear for generations among the Jewish Priests, as did the Brahminical teaching before it was reduced to writing,--yet we do not find the Jewish rites as elaborate as those practiced by other nations. The Jewish Kabbalistic doctrines were not written down until the first century of our era. Rabbi Eleazar, the son of Rabbi Simeon Ben Jochai, compiled the Kabbalistic teaching of his father into a work called the Zohar, but these teachings did not originate with that noted Rabbi, they reach far into remote antiquity.

This book, which was edited between 70 and 100 A. D., was lost, and its, sacred contents were preserved only in a number of scattered manuscripts.

The Zohar was rewritten, according to Munk, by Moses de Leon, in the 13th century, and was based upon those fragmentary manuscripts and ancient documents which have been partially destroyed or lost to the general world.

The Sepher Jetzerah (or Jewish Book of Creation) is first mentioned in the 10th century, although its contents are very ancient. These two books, the Zohar and Jetzerah, are the storehouse of all subsequent Kabbalistic works.

The Kabbalistic writings, then, are comparatively modern, but their doctrines came to the Jews from the Chaldeans and Egyptians. Moses was an Initiate, and knew the primitive universal mystery-language, also the numerical system on which it was based, but his writings have not come down to us-- the books attributed to him are not the original Mosaic Records.

The early Hebrew teachings derived from Moses had various fortunes--the original scrolls were probably lost and rewritten many times before the days of Ezra, and when the Jews were carried away into captivity, the Jewish Scriptures were destroyed. Ezra endeavored to restore them as best he could, but they have been tampered with even since his day. The Samaritans repudiate the Jewish canonical books. They are disfigured, they say, beyond all recognition by the Talmudists. They have their books of Moses, differing materially, yet claimed by the Samaritans to be carefully copied from the original.

The Black Jews of Southern India know nothing of the captivity, thus proving that they emigrated previous to 600 B. C. They also have a Book of Moses which differs greatly from either of the above canonical books.

Although the Jews are right in declaring that Moses originally gave them their cosmology and laws, still the records of these laws have been so changed that the present books attributed to him are not the original books at all. Some fragments of the earlier writings and traditions may have been available at the time of Ezra, but in all probability the main allegories were taken from the symbolical records of the Chaldeans, as the earlier allegories had been adopted from similar records in Egypt.

The doctrine of the Kabbalah is practically the same as that of the ancient universal teaching. Ain Soph is the western and Semitic Parabrahman. Between the Absolute Ain Soph and the Heavenly Man, there is an impersonal

First Cause. Dr Ginsburg says, "For to reveal itself to us, the concealed of all the concealed sent forth the Ten Emanations ( Sephoroth) called the Form of God, Form of the Heavenly Man. Yet since even this luminous form was too dazzling for our vision, it had to put on another garment, which is the universe. The universe, therefore, or the visible world, is a further expression of the Divine Substance, and is called in the Kabbalah, The Garment of God." This is the doctrine of the Vishnu Parana and in fact of all the schools.

But it is not my purpose here to expound the teaching of the Mysteries, so we must forego further comment.

The Kabbalah is of value in throwing light upon the exoteric Hebrew books, although it has been so changed that it cannot be trusted to reveal the ancient teaching unless corroborated by other data.

In the early times there was a company of prophets at Naioth, Bethel, and Jericho, who formed schools of Initiates where the secret teaching was imparted to those wh‚o were qualified to hear. These schools of the prophets were also schools for the development of the higher psychic and spiritual faculties, while in later times the Essenes, Theraputes, and other communities, were the repositories of the occult Jewish teaching. It will be interesting here to consider these well known sects.

THE ESSENES.

For some centuries before the Christian era the Essenean communities dwelt on the shores of the Dead Sea. Their chief characteristic was the doctrine of love - love of God, love of virtue, and love of human kind. They lived a life of ascetic communism in which certain hours were devoted to the study of religion-- the mysteries of nature and revelation. They had an inner instruction, an occult teaching, which was guarded with great secrecy. They were evidently in contact with Chaldean Kabbalism as they made much of the mysteries connected with the Tetragrammaton, the four lettered mystic name of Deity.

The Essenes had their degrees and Initiations, in which we find the identity of teaching between Essenism and Christianity is most marked. Mr. Mead sums up these points of contact somewhat as follows: Converts were required to sell their posessions and give to the poor, for the laying up of treasure was regarded as injurious to a spiritual life. Not only did the Essenes despise riches, but they lived a life of self-imposed poverty. Love of the brotherhood and of one's neighbor was the soul of Essene life, and the basis of all action; and this characteristic of their discipline called forth universal admiration. The members lived together as a family, had all things in common, and appointed a

steward to manage the common purse. When traveling they would lodge with brethren whom they had never seen before, as though with the oldest and most intimate friends; and thus they took nothing with them when they went on a journey. All members were on the same level, and the authority of one over another was forbidden; nevertheless mutual service was mutually enjoined. They were also great lovers of peace, and so refused to take arms or manufacture warlike weapons; moreover they proscribed slavery. The ultimate aim of the Essenes was to be meek and lowly in spirit, to mortify all sinful lusts, to be pure in heart, to hate evil but reclaim the evil doer, and to be merciful to all men and moreover, their yea was to be yea, and their nay, nay. They were devoted to the curing of the sick and the healing of both body and soul, regarding the power to perform miraculous cures and cast out evil spirits as the highest stage of discipline. In brief, they strove to be so pure as to become temples of the Holy Spirit, and thus seers and prophets. To these inner communities were attached outer circles of pupils living in the world, and found in all the main centres of the Diaspora. (Fragments of a Faith Forgotten, Mead, p. 134.)

The Therapeutes were practically the same as the Essenes with the exception, pointed out by Philo, that the latter were devoted to the practical life, while the former proceeded to the higher stages of the contemplative life.

It would be interesting, did time permit. to give a full account of these Therapeutist communities, which were so like early Christianity that the Church Fathers always recognized them as Christians. Philo in his "Contemplative Life," gives a full description of these "Wisdom Lovers." Through their yearning for the blessed life they abandoned the world and sought some secluded spot, and gave themselves entirely to study and contemplation. In Egypt there were many in every Province, and especially around Alexandria. The most advanced joined the Mareotic colony, which was situated just south of Alexandria on a small plateau. The dwellings of this community were very simple, each containing a small chamber or closet in which, in solitude, they performed the mysteries of the holy life.

Philo would lead us to believe that the Therapeutes were all Jews. This was probably true of the Mareotic community with which he was connected as lay pupil, but this was only one of a vast number of such communities scattered all over the world. It is quite probable that many of these were as strongly tinged with Egyptian or Zoroastrian or Orphic elements as the one south of Alexandria was with Judalsm. Many of these communities were purely eclectic--combining traditions and elements

of the various schools. THE PHARISEES.

We are fairly familiar with the external side of Phariseeism--the minute ceremonialism and elaborate rules of external piety--but the inner side is not so well understood. The most learned of the Jews belonged to this sect, which originated in Babylon, and represented the main stream of Chaldean and Persian influence on Judaism. In the course of time it became divided into many schools, the strictest of which led a life of internal piety. The highest aim of this school was to attain to such a state of holiness, as to be able to perforrn miraculous cures and to prophesy. The degrees of holiness practiced by this sect are given by Mr. Mead as follows: (I.) the study of the law and circumspection; ( II.) the noviciate, in which the apron was a symbol of purity; (III.) external purity, by means of lustrations or baptisms; (IV.) celibacy; (V.) inward purity, purity of thought; (VI.) a still higher stage, which is not further defined; (VII.) meekness and holiness; (VIII.) dread of every sin; (IX.) the highest stage of holiness; (X.) the stage which enabled the adept to heal the sick and raise the dead. (Ibid, p. I33.)

It is quite evident that there was a wide difference between the tenets of the Healers and the other Pharisees who believed in the blood sacrifices of the Temple-worship and the resurrection of the physical body. This again illustrates the difference between the exoteric and esoteric cults.

All these mystic schools constituted links in the chain of the Wisdom or Gnosis transmission. Jesus himself taught nothing new, he merely illuminated the traditions of the Gnosis, and in his public teaching practically threw open to all some of the intermediate grades of the Mysteries. The Jews, then, in common with all the ancient nations, were in possession of an occult teaching, which is the same old Wisdom Religion, that has ever stood as the background of the popular religious systems.

The distinction sometimes made between religions--that the Jewish and Christian are pure, and that the Pagan is spurious, is an error due to a very narrow conception. The higher criticism and recent study of comparative religions has shown us that we can no longer hold to the belief in one perfect supernatural religion, condemning all others as false. That God left the world to wander in darkness until two, three or four thousand years ago is contradicted by every Sage, and by the great body of religious literature that preceded the Jewish and Christian eras. God is no respecter of persons, therefore no religion has a

monopoly of truth. Each great World-Faith has a part to play in the Divine Economy. While we recognize Jesus as the great Initiate and Messenger to the Western world, let us not ignore the other Divine Teachers whom God has sent as Messengers from the same Great Lodge. The same Wisdom illuminated them all--they are all kindred and belong to the same Great Brotherhood.

Limited time has prevented me from going into greater details regarding the ceremonies of Initiation. Enough, however, has been said to bear out the fact that all the Mysteries of antiquity have a common origin. They bear the most striking resemblance to each other both in ceremonies and doctrines. Thus, we have seen that Initiations in all the Mysteries were set forth in a Mystery-Myth, sometimes called the Sun-Myth, which in its various settings symbolizes the activity of the Logos, on the one hand, and the mystic life of the Initiate on the other. The hero of the myth, representing the Solar Logos and the Perfect Initiate, was known by different names in different countries-- Osiris-Horus in Egypt, Ormazd-Mithra in Persia,

Zeus-Hermes in Greece, Jupiter-Ammon in Rome, Thor-Balder in Britain and Scandinavia.

The Initiates knew the real meaning of these Myths, for literally the Sun is not born and does not die, nor is it raised from the dead. The recitals of these events are allegories, which veil a deeper truth. In the popular religions the Sun became the object of worship, and the Hero of the Myths became the God of the various religions when the symbol was mistaken for ihe thing symbolized. The Myth is an allegory of the activity of the Logos in the Cosmos, and of the various stages of Initiation, and like all the rites, it typifies the mystic life of every Initiate. Every perfected Master becomes a Christ, a Hermest etc. Initiation consists in attaining the Master-state. A failure to understand these symbols and allegories resulted in the crude dogmas of popular theology. Many have read this later thought into the Mysteries themselves, and have supposed that the rites merely symbolized the death and resurrection of some Hero or Demi-God-- some special divine personage who was considered by the celebrants as a God. According to this the aspirant was merely representing the death and resurrection of the God from whom the Mysteries derived their name. This crude conception falls far short of the reality, for the cosmic aspect of all these religious tragedies was symbolized by the activity of the Logos in the universe, but these Sun-Myths also typify the mystic life of the Initiate. The Initiate did not merely represent some Hero, he was the Hero himself, and the rites typified what he became--a Buddha, a Christ, a Mithra, etc., one whose mystic life represented the mystic lives of all who had previously trod the path, though that was not the primary significance of the

ceremony.

Perhaps after the Mysteries became corrupt and degraded, so-called Initiates might have mis-read the allegories and symbols, but such was not the case in the days of the real Initiates--before the key to the Sacred Science was lost.

The use of the image, in some instances employed to represent the candidate, evidently came into use when the Institution had become so changed that the candidate objected to being laid away in the tomb, as was originally the custom, and another indication of decIine was the physical terror to which the candidate was subjected. This was to test his courage and was supposed to illustrate the experiences he would meet in the invisible world.

In the early days, we are told, the candidate was entranced when laid away in the tomb, he then actually visited the invisible world and encountered the grotesque images and forms to be seen there. He was taught the "words of power" and the "signs of power," although they were only a means of strengthening the will, which alone, however, is sufficient to overcome the phantomed terrors. The Hierophant also used his occult power to materialize illustrations of various postmortem conditions.

That the Mysteries were designed to reveal the invisible world, is clearly stated by Plutarch, who was himself an Initiate of high standing. He says that when a man dies he goes through the same experiences as those who have their consciousness increased in the Mysteries. Thus in the terms, 'to die' and 'to be Initiated' we have an exact correspondence, word to word and fact to fact. First of all there are wanderings and weary journeyings and paths on which we look with suspicion, and that seem to have no termination; then, before the end, every kind of terror, shuddering, trembling, sweating, stupor. But at last a marvelous light shines out to meet us, pure scenes and fair fields welcome us, with song and dance and the solemnities of sacred sounds and holy sights.
In which state he who has already perfected himself in
all things, and received Initiation, accomplishes his mystery, reaches his full freedom, and passing everywhere at will, he receives the crown, and is in communion with the holy and pure; now gazing down upon the unpurified multitude of the uninitiated who are still in life, wallowing in the deep mire and mist, and abiding in misery from fear of death and want of faith in the blessedness of the soul-life. (Plut. Frag. V. 9 ed. Didot.)
The vision of Aridaeus, also given by Plutarch was, according to Mead, either a literary subterfuge for

describing some of the instruction in certain Mysteries, or a partial description of the invisible world and the conditions of the soul after death, although, as we have said, the former was a revelation of the latter. But when the power to directly reveal the future state was lost, they had to illustrate it by dramatic and scenic representations. To produce the ghostly images and phantoms in the physical plane Mysteries, actors, and even mirrors were often used-- not as a deception, however, for everybody understood that these were illustrations only.

With the loss of the higher means of revelation, corruption gradually crept in ard man at last was left to win his deliverance without the visible aid of the Great Teachers, yet we are assured by wise preceptors that those great souls remain constant, even though unseen, and are ever ready to aid and assist the needy whenever they comply with the great occult law of the universe.

## THE DECLINE OF THE MYSTERIES.

The cause of the decline of the Mysteries was the personal ambition of crafty priests and despotic rulers. They began to lose this grandeur and glory before the days of Aristotle, their retrogression, however, was gradual; for at the time of Cicero they retained much of their early sanctity and purity, and even as late as the time of Nero, for as unscrupulous as he became he did not dare to aid in the celebration of the Mysteries after commiting a hideous crime. The great occult knowledge which had moved westward for thousands of years began about 500 B. C. to recede to its Eastern source.

Owing to the Ethiopian invasion 570 B. C., the royal throne fell into the hands of Amases, a man of low birth, who destroyed the priestly order. It is not strange, that in the decadence of Greece and Rome, even the Mysteries should share in the general degradation. Selfishness ruled with an iron hand and before the end of the Roman Empire, the true spirit of the Mysteries was withheld, leaving only the outer forms behind. It would be unfair to judge the real Mysteries from the relics of this period.

The last of the Pagan Mysteries in Europe disappeared with the destruction of the great cities of Gaul -- Alesia, Bibractis and Arles, and although the great world-wide institution nearly perished except in the East, the secret doctrine was not lost, nor entirely abandoned even in the West. It is quite a task to follow it through the shifting religious life of the Middle Ages, but recent investigations have shown that it has been unbrokenly continued in secret fraternities from age to age. We shall trace this descent in a future lecture.

5

LECTURE IV

THE CHRISTIAN MYSTERIES.
THE TESTIMONY OF JESUS AND THE APOSTLES.

The Christian Religion, in common with all the great religions of antiquity, originally possessed an inner or occult teaching.

W.J.B. MacLeod Moore 33d, Supreme Grand Master "Ad Vitam" of the Sovereign Priory of Canada, United Orders of the Temple of Malta, says: "The secrets of the Mystery of Christianity were only communicated to the Initiates, and these Initiates were first made Christians, then advanced in Christianity, and finally raised to a knowledge of all its Aporrheta. There were three degrees or steps in Christianity,and its religious system was known as the 'Disciplina Arcana'-- the discipline of the secret. There was an esoteric and exoteric doctrine. The three classes who received the three degrees of the primitive church were the 'Catechumens,' the 'Competentes,' and the 'Illuminati.' In the first degree of Christianity the candidate was baptized. Baptism introduced the believer to the Christian Mystery. The sacred doctrines taught in the several degrees were those of the 'Trinity in Unity,' the 'Incarnation of the Logos or Son of God,' 'the Crucifixion,' 'the Resurrection,' and the 'Secret of the Liturgy.' Baptism initiated the candidate, while a participation in the Lord's Supper, or Eucharist, marked the raising of the candidate to the highest degree of Christian light and doctrine. All through the writings of the early Fathers of the Church reference is made to the Christian Mysteries and their secret doctrines. Initiates were strictly forbidden to paint, cut or carve any reference to them." (History of

Freemasonry and Concordant Orders, p. 746.)
Before we examine the records to see if this contention can be substantiated, let us first note something of the Christian movement. The origin of Christianity is involved in great obscurity. Even the period at which Jesus lived is a matter of controversy. The following occult account accords with the Talmud in stating that Jesus lived in the days of King Jannai, who reigned over the Jews 104 to 78 B. C., and is as follows: "The child whose Jewish name has been turned into that of Jesus was born in Palestine, B.C. 105, during the consulate of Publicus Rutilus Rufus and Gnaeus Mallius Maximus. His parents were well-born though poor, and he was educated in a knowledge of the Hebrew Scriptures.
His fervent devotion and a gravity beyond his years led his parents to dedicate him to the religious and ascetic life, and, soon after a visit to Jerusalem, in

which the extraordinary intelligence and eagerness for knowledge of the youth were shown in his seeking of the doctors in the Temple, he was sent to be trained in an Essene community in the southern Judean desert. When he had reached the age of nineteen he went on to the Essene Monastery near Mount Serbal, a monastery which was much visited by learned men traveling from Persia and India to Egypt, and where a magnificent library of occult works--many of them Indian of the Trans-Himalayan regions--had been established. From this seat of mystic learning he proceeded later to Egypt. He had been fully instructed in the secret teachings which were the real fount of life among the Essenes, and was initiated in Egypt as a disciple of that one Sublime Lodge from which every great religion has its Founder. For Egypt has remained one of the world centres of the true Mysteries, whereof all semi-public Mysteries are the faint and far-off reflections. The Mysteries spoken of in history as Egyptian, were the shadows of the true things 'in the Mount,' and there the young Hebrew received the solemn consecration which prepared him for the Royal Priesthood he was later to attain." (Esoteric Christianity Besant, p. 128 & 129.)

The time having come for the founding of a new religion, a suitable tabernacle was needed for the Great Teacher who was to be sent into the world. Jesus offered his body as a willing sacrifice. One called the Christ took possession of Jesus' body at the age of 29, and for two years instructed the heads of the Essene communities, and for one year he taught the general public. It is only of the last year's work that some tradition is preserved for us in the Gospel story. He was finally rejected by the Essenes because he carried to the outer world some portions of the spiritual wisdom which they regarded as their exclusive possession. The clouds of hatred thickened until finally the body of Jesus paid the penalty for enshrining the Great Teacher. But the Master did not forget his promise to return to his, chosen disciples, and for some fifty years he visited them in his spiritual body, and continued his instruction in the secret teaching. This inner instruction constituted the basis of the Christian Mysteries. During this time the disciples lived together in a re- tired spot on the outskirts of Judea, attracting small attention because of the many similar communities. During its embryonic stage the new religion was hidden in the womb of communities, similar to that of the Therapeutes. It was, some years before it emerged and began its general propaganda, and it was only when the disciples were fully prepared that they went forth to preach.

After Jesus' death he completed his human evolution and became a Perfect Master. The Christ then surrendered to Jesus the care of the Christian Church, and He became

the Hierophant in the Christian Mysteries. He was the inspiration that kept alive the Gnosis in the Church until the mass of ignorant selfish- ness became too great for its continuance. But he has sought through- out the centuries, and is seeking to-day, for those who have eyes to see and ears to hear Wisdom. (For full exposition see "Esoteric Christianity," Besant, Ch. IV.)

This is the occult teaching, which is, fully corroborated by the doctrine of the early Gnostics. They held that those whom Christ originally instructed in the higher doctrines, brought about his condemnation for blasphemy by the Orthodox Jewish authorities, because they considered that his too open teaching was a divulgence of the Mysteries. They also held, as can be seen by consulting the Pistis Sophia, written by Valentinus, that after Jesus' death he continued his instruction of the disciples. For eleven years he taught them so far as "the regions of the first statues only and up to the regions of the first mystery, the mystery within the veil." Notwithstanding, there were omissions of many points which as yet they were unable to comprehend, the instruction was so wonderful that they thought that all had been revealed, the gnosis of all gnoses. In the twelfth year, having received the robe of glory, he says to his disciples "Lo, I have put on My vesture, and all power hath been given Me by the First Mystery. Yet a little while and I will tell you the mystery of the pleroma and the pleroma of the pleroma; I will conceal nothing from you from this hour, but in perfectness will I perfect you in the whole pleroma, and all perfection, and every mystery; which things, indeed, are the perfection, of all perfections, the pleroma of all pleroma, and the gnosis of all gnoses, which are in My vesture. I will tell you all mysteries from the exterior of the exteriors, to the interior of the interiors." This the Master did and instructed them in the Mystery of the First Mystery and the Mystery of the Ineffable. Then follows instruction on the nature of the preaching by the disciples when the Master has entered the Light, and the condition upon which the Mysteries shall be given to others. He then teaches them regarding the postmortem state of the sinner, the righteous uninitiated, and the righteous initiated, etc. This secret teaching constituted the Mysteries of Jesus.

The public and private teaching of Jesus naturally resulted in two traditions. The mystic tradition represents the inner teaching, and the Ebionite represents the public teaching. It was against the original followers of the public tradition that Paul contended his efforts to universalize Christianity. The Petro-Pauline controversy was a struggle between the external and mystic sides of the new movement. The Ebionites undoubtedly preserved the original and true

tradition regarding the birth and nature of Jesus, for they held that Jesus was a man born as other men, the natural son of Joseph and Mary. That the tradition of the Ebionites or Nazarcens differed widely from the historicized dogmas of later times, may be seen, even to-day, from the Codex Nasarceus of the Mandaites, the descendants of the Nazarceans who dwell in the marshes of Southern Babylonia. We must not confuse the early form of Ebionitism with the later forms which were of a Gnostic nature--the outer communities being finally influenced by the inner Jewish tradition.

Paul himself was a mystic, in touch with the inner communities, and he saw that Christianity was designed to be the religion of the new race about to be born. It is evident that Paul was not acquainted with the later accounts of the canonical Gospels, for he does not teach the historical Jesus, but the Mystic Christ. The canonical accounts were probably compiled in the last quarter of the first century or in the first part of the second, that is, they reached their present form at that time. The synoptics were based upon a sketch of an ideal life, written by one of the Apostles of the inner communities, and intended for general circulation.

Round this nucleus, later compilers, bishops of the outer churches, wove much other matter which was selected from a mass of legend and tradition. Orthodoxy or General Christianity traces its origin to these documents.

We are now ready to examine the teachings of Jesus and the Apostles, and see if we can find any trace or reference to an inner occult teaching. Upon reading an account of Jesus' teaching we find him constantly making use of certain terms which are usually employed to designate an inner circle of Initiation.

In the fourth chapter of Mark is recorded the parable of the sower, given by Jesus to the multitude, at the conclusion of which he said, "He that hath ears to hear let him hear." "And when he was alone," the writer says, "they that were about him with the twelve asked of him the parable," and He said unto them, "Unto you it is given to know the mystery of the kingdom of God; but unto them that are without, all these things are done in parables." (Mark, IV., 9, 10, 11). A little later in the same chapter we are told, "With many such parables spake He the word unto them, as they were able to hear it. But without a parable spake he not unto them, and when they were alone he expounded all things to his disciples." (Ibid, 33, 34.) The writer records the intellectual interpretation of the parable of the sower given by Jesus to his disciples. These things have a three-fold meaning--a surface, an intellectual interpretation, and a mystical or spiritual meaning, which was never written but was committed orally by the teacher to his pledged disciple. Origen says all

Scripture has a body, the common historical sense; a soul, a figurative meaning to be intellectually discerned; and a spirit, an inner occult sense, known only to the spiritually minded. It was this inner occult teaching that Jesus gave to those "in the house when they were alone,"-- to those who were privileged to "know the mysteries of the kingdom of God."

The Kingdom of Heaven or Kingdom of God refers to the Mystery-Institution or to the spiritual state which, the discipline and Kowledge or Gnosis revealed in the Mysteries, enabled one to attain. In the Pistis Sophia Jesus is said to have brought the "Keys of the Mysteries of the Kingdom of Light," meaning that the perfect Initiate had attained the Kingdom, the high spiritual state, even while on earth. In the "Book of the Great Logos," another early Gnostic treatise, we are told that those who have received the Greater Mysteries, the Mysteries of the Light Treasure, "have already inherited the Kingdom of God while still on earth; they have their share in the Light Treasure and are immortal Gods."

We see by this the real meaning of Jesus' saying, "Give not that which is holy to the dogs, neither cast ye your pearls before swine." (Matt. VII., 6.) "Dogs" like "the vulgar" and "the profane" was a term applied by those within a certain circle, to all who were on the outside. This was the sense in which Jesus used the terms; for those not initiated into the mysteries of the knowledge could not understand the inner teaching; and to give it to them would be like casting pearls before swine.

Again the names "Kingdom," the "Kingdom of God" or the "Kingdom of Heaven," the "Strait Gate" the "Narrow Way," the "Saved," are all technical terms connected with Initiation and the Mysteries. This is evident from the passages in which these terms occur. The question was asked Jesus, "Are there few that be saved?" and he replied, "Strive to enter in at the strait gate: for many, I say unto you, will seek to enter in, and shall not be abIe." (Luke XIII, 23, 24) Again, he said, "Enter ye in at the strait gate: for wide is the gate, and broad is the way, that leadeth to destruction, and many there be which go in thereat: because strait is the gate, and narrow is the way, which leadeth unto life, and few there be that find it." (Matt., VII, 13, 14.)

The application of this passage to the future world is without foundation. To suppose that many will earnestly seek to enter heaven but will be unable to gain admission is both unreasonable and unscriptural. When the Seer of the Apocalypse describes the heavenworld he does not behold merely a few, but a "great multitude which no man could number." (Rev VII., 9.)

The "Strait Gate" here is not the gateway of heaven, but the gateway of Initiation. Few, indeed, have succeeded in entering this "Strait Gate," although many have sought its portals. There are some, even to-day, who can bear witness to this statement, some who for years have striven but have not yet reached the goal.

The "Saved," the true Initiates, thase who have attained the "Kingdom," or spiritual Nirvana, have always been few. Some three thousand years earlier, Krishna said, "Among thousands of men, scarce one striveth for perfection; of the successful strivers scarce one knoweth me in essence." The great multitude have always followed the broad way which leadeth time and again to destruction; only the few have sought the narrower and steeper road of Initiation that leadeth direct unto life.

The student of the worlds' Scriptures is familiar with the symbol of the "Narrow Way." It is the old narrow way so often referred to, the "Path difficult to tread as the edge of a razor." Jesus does not use the symbol in any new sense. It is the old "Strait Gate" and "Narrow Way" of Initiation. This was symbolized in the Ancient Mysteries by the narrow stone orifice which separated each of the seven caverns from its successor, and through which the candidate had to pass in going from one chamber to the next. The Kings Chamber in the great Pyramid was entered through such a gate.

Regarding this Mr. Stansland Wake says, "The so-called King's Chamber.... was probably the place to which the Initiate was admitted after he had gone through the narrow upward passage, and the grand gallery with its

lowly terrnination which gradually prepared him for the final stage of the Sacred Mysteries." (Origin and Significance of the Great Pyramids," p. 93.) This passage symbolized the "Narrow" or "Strait Gate" which "leadeth unto life"--the new spiritual rebirth--to which Jesus referred. It was a symbol, the meaning of which was well understood by every Initiate. The Mason will recall a similar symbol in the gateway through which he passed in the Royal Arch Degree.

It is of interest to note, in this connection, the incident of the young man who came to Jesus and addressing him said, "Good Master, what good thing shall I do that I may have eternal Life?" He wished to secure a permanent abode in that world where they die no more, in other words, he was seeking liberation from the necessity of repeated births and deaths. Remember, the Jews believed that all imperfect souls returned to earth life. In reply Jesus gave the usual exoteric answer, "Keep the commandments." But when the young man said he had kept all these from his youth up, Jesus said to him, "If wilt be perfect, go and sell that thou hath and give to the poor and thou shalt have treasure in heaven and come and follow me." (Matt. XIX., 21.)

To be "Perfect" is to attain a certain stage of Initiation. Jesus here uses a technical term, the meaning of which was well known at that time. The Essenes used the term to denote a certain class in their communites. They had three divisons--the Neophytes, the Brethren and the Perfect. If thou wilt be "Perfect," a member of the Kingdom, you must comply with the conditions--poverty and obedience. Such has always been a condition for Initiation. When the young man heard the necessity of this he went away sorrowful; for he had great possessions. Jesus then turned to his disciples and moralized upon the difficulties that stand in the way of a rich man entering upon the higher stages of human evolution, saying, "It is easier for a camel to go through the eye of a needle, than for a rich man to enter the Kingdom of God. (Ibid 24.) To apply this to the future state is absurd. Does anyone really believe that no rich man can enter heaven ?

There seems to be no great haste in getting rid of

riches on account of the text. But when we understand that the "Kingdom of Heaven" means the "Brotherhood of the Initiated," we see at once that the statement is literally true. One cannot gain that knowledge of God which is eternal life, the condition of the "Perfect," while engrossed with the cares of great wealth. It is only when one is stripped of these cares and anxieties, incident upon the possession of great riches and vast interests in the material world, that he can pass the narrow gateway of the world of the spirit. Poverty, obedience, and chastity were the vows taken by the candidate for Initiation in all ages, and Jesus simply repeats the universal teaching.

Another indication of Jesus' knowledge of the technical terms of Initiation is in the words spoken to Nicodemus, "Verily, verily, I say unto thee, Except a man be born again, he cannot see the Kingdom of God." (John III, 3.) This birth or baptism is spoken of as of water and of the spirit, the first baptism is the first Initiation, when the candidate is welcomed as a "little child." There was a later Initiation, the baptism of the Initiate in his manhood, called the baptlsm of the Holy Ghost and fire. (Matt. III, II.)

In the Codex Nasarceus of the Mandaites there is a beautiful story of this mystic baptism. Jesus comes to Johannah to be baptized--seeking Initiation into the the mystic school of Johannah. But Johannah recognizes him as the Master by whose power he had been teaching and initiating for forty and two years. Johannah gives the lower Initiation of external Baptism to Jesus, and receives in turn the true spiritual baptism from the Master himself, when "He gave him the grip of the Rushta, and laid his hand upon him in Jordan; and He made him lay off his garment of flesh and blood; and He clothed him in a raiment of glory." The phrases "little

ones," "little child" and "children." were used in the mystic circles of the time to denote one just Initiated. Johannah says, "Come in peace, Little One.... Now, I go with thee, Little One, that we may enter the stream.... Come. come, Little One of three years and one day, youngest among his brethren but oldest with his Father, who is so small yet his sayings are so exalted." In the Essene and Therapeute communities senority was reckoned not by age, but by the years the brother had been a member of the Order.

The "Second Birth" is also a well recognized and universal term for Initiatlon. This will be clearly seen when we consider more definitely the question of Initiation in a succeeding lecture.

On the night preceding his death, Jesus said to his Apostles, "I have yet many things to say unto you, but ye cannot bear them now." ( John XVI, 12.) Some of these things were undoubtedly said by Jesus after his resurrection, during the period when he remained with his disciples, "Speaking to them of the things pertaining to the Kingdom of God." Of course, none of these things pertaining, as they did, to the "Kingdom of God"--the Mysteries--are publicly recorded; but one cannot doubt that they were treasured and handed down orally as a precious heritage. There is a tradition in the early church that this instruction continued, not only forty days, but for many years.

We will now turn to St. Paul. We shall find the writings of this Apostle to the Gentiles permeated with references to occult teachings and the Mysteries; his use of the technical terms connected with Initiation is sufficient to prove, to any unprejudiced mind, the existence of the inner teaching of the Church in its primitive state.

In the first Epistle to the Corinthians, Paul refers to the degree of "Perfection" and to the teaching that belongs to that degree; he says, "We speak wisdom among them that are perfect. . . We speak the wisdom of God in a mystery, even the hidden wisdom which God ordained before the world unto our glory: which none of the princes of this world knew. . . But God hath revealed them unto us by his spirit: for the spirit searcheth all things, yea, the deep things of God. . . Which things also we speak, not in the words which man's wisdom teacheth but which the Holy Ghost teacheth." (I Cor. II, 6, 7, 10, 13.)
"And I, brethren, could not speak unto you as unto spiritual, but as unto carnal, even as unto babes in Christ. I have fed you with milk, and not with meat; for hitherto ye were not able to bear it, neither yet now are ye able. For ye are yet carnal.... As a wise master-builder, I have laid the foundation." (I Cor. III., 1, 2, 3, 10.)


"Let a man so account of us, as of the ministers of Christ, and stewards of the mysteries of God." (I Cor. IV, I.)
Is it not evident from these passages that the Apostle possessed an inner wisdom that the Christians at Corinth were not yet able to receive ? Remember that these words were addressed to those who were in full membership of the Church. They had all that the modern church gives to its members, but there was a hidden wisdom which they could not yet bear. This wisdom was only given in the Mysteries--where wisdom was spoken among the "Perfect." The recurring technical terms in these passages should evidence their connection with the world-wide Mysteries: The "Perfect," the "Wisdom," the "Hidden Wisdom," the "Wisdom of God in a Mystery," the "wise Master-builder," "Stewards of the Mysteries of God"--Paul constantly uses these technical terms which be-

long to the mystic tradition. The communities which he addressed must have been familiar with his nomenclature, for he does not speak of these things as new, but as well known to those to whom he writes.

In the Epistle to the Ephesians Paul refers to the Mysteries. saying that by "revelation he made known unto me the mystery," "my knowledge in the mystery of Christ" that all men might see the "fellowship of the mystery." (Eph. III, 3, 4, 9.)
In the Epistle to the Colossians, Paul declares that he had been made a minister to fulfill the word of God, "Even the mystery which hath been hid from ages and from generations, but now is made manifest to his saints: To whom God would make known what is the riches of the glory of this mystery among the Gentiles; which is Christ in you, the hope of glory." (Col. I, 26-27.) This Christ within is indeed a mystery--it is the life of the Initiate, which, when fully developed, will present the man "perfect In Jesus Christ."
In the Epistle to the Philippians Paul says, "I count all things but loss for the excellency of the knowledge of Christ Jesus. . . That I may know him, and the power of his resurrection, and the fellowship of his sufferings, being made conformable unto his death: If by any means I might attain unto the resurrection of the dead. Not as though I had already attained, either were already perfect. . . Let us therefore, as many as be perfect, be thus minded." (Phil. III, 8-15.)
The resurrection which the Apostle was striving to attain was not the ordinary resurrection of Christian belief, for this requires no effort. But there is a "resurrection" which is not easily attained. Jesus refers to this in his reply to the Sadducees, "But they which shall be accounted worthy to obtain that world,

and the resurrection from the dead, neither marry nor are given in marriage: neither can they die any more: far they are equal unto the angels; and are children of God, being the children of the resurrection." (Luke XX, 35, 36.)
Jesus here connects the resurrection with liberation from death--those

attaining the resurrection "do not die any more." The perfected Initiate was liberated from the "circle of generations" of birth and death, he was worthy to obtain that world of permanent abode. The real man is sexless and those who are able to abandon their animal nature, return to the eternal essence above, where there is neither male nor female, but a new creature--this is the true resurrection. When the neophyte reached a certain stage of interior development or enlightment he was said to "rise from the dead." The phrase "resurrection from the dead" is a mystical phrase denoting the new birth or Gnostic Illumination. The Apostle was striving to attain that resurrection, and he urges "as many as are perfect" to strive also. He does not urge the ordinary believer; for only those who had attained to the degree of the "Perfect" could hope for immediate deliverance. He was already of the "Perfect" and he says to his fellow Initiates, "I press toward the mark for the prize of the high calling of God in Christ Jesus. Let us, therefore, as many as be perfect, be thus minded." The Initiate was to become the Risen Christ. "The ordinary believer had put on Christ.... They were babes in Christ.... Christ was the Savior to whom they looked for help, knowing Him after the flesh. But when they had conquered the lower nature and were no longer 'carnal,' then they were to enter on a higher path, and were themselves to become Christ." (Esoteric Christianity, Besant, p. 63.)

Paul had struggled to attain this ideal and had at last succeeded. He says, "I am now ready to be offered, and the time of my departure is at hand. I have fought a good fight, I have finished my course, I have kept the faith; henceforth there is laid up for me a crown of righteousness." (II Timothy, IV, 6-8.. "This was the crown given 'to him that overcometh,' of whom it is said by the ascended Christ: 'I will make him a pillar in the temple of my God; and he shall go no more out." (Rev. III, 12.) For after the Resurrection the Initiate has become the Perfect Man, the Master, and He goes out no more from the Temple." (Esoteric Christianity, p. 65.)

In the First Epistle to Timothy, Paul exhorts his son in the faith to see that nothing is done contrary to sound doctrine. Paul declares that the glorious gospel of the blessed God has been committed to his trust, and he commits to Timothy an important charge in this connection. "This charge I commit unto thee, son

Timothy." (I Timothy, I., 18.) And again he says, "O Timothy, keep that which is committed to thy trust." (Ibid VI., 20.) "Hold fast the form of sound words which thou hast heard of me....that good thing which was committed unto thee, keep by the Holy Ghost which dwelleth in us." (II Timothy I., 13, 14.) "Neglect not the gift that is in thee, which was given thee by prophecy, with the laying on of the hands of the Presbytery"--of the Initiates. (I Timothy IV., 14.) This knowledge which had been committed to Timothy and which he was to guard so completely, was not the common kowledge possessed by Christians in general, there was no special obligations laid upon him regarding that, but it was the doctrine committed to his trust as an Initiate.

Paul instructs him to select deacons frorn among those who had a knowledge of the "mystery of the Faith," and the "mystery of godliness." He was further to provide for the transmission of this sacred teaching, "the things that thou hast heard of me among many witnesses [in the assembly of Initiates], the same cornmit thou to faithful men, who shall be able to teach others also." (II. Timothy, II, 2.) This, of course, refers to the sacred oral teachings given only to Initiates. If the ordinary doctrines of the church were meant, Timothy would have been instructed to write it down for transmission, or rather Paul would have written it out himself. But the secret teaching could not be written; they were not the things read by Timothy, they were Paul's private instructions, given within the sacred precincts; they were to be transmitted to others by word of mouth. Paul initiates Timothy into the Mysteries of the Church, and exhorts him to "keep that which is coqnmitted to his trust," and to provide for the due transmission of this knowledge to other teachers. We thus have provision made for the transmission of the occult wisdom for three

generations--Timothy represents the generation of Christian teachers immediately following the Apostles, and he is instructed to commit the hidden treasure to faithful men who shall teach others in turn.

We now refer to the writings of the Apostolic Fathers, and we shall not be surprised to find that they possessed an esoteric teaching, for the provision made by Paul overlaps the early part of this period. In-our next we will consider the testimony of the early Church.

## 6

## LECTURE V

THE CHRISTIAN MYSTERIES.
( Concluded.)
TESTIMONY OF THE EARLY CHURCH.

In the last lecture we examined the testimonies of Christ and His Apostles, and found that they had an inner teaching, a deep spiritual knowledge, which was not imparted to the masses.

We shall now proceed to the history of the early church in which we find that the Mysteries, as established by Christ, constituted a definite institution in the early Christian centuries.

There were two traditions of the Christian Gnosis --the Gnostic, which recognized the Christian Gnosis as only a part of the General Gnosis, and the orthodox, which held to the exclusive character of the Christian Gnosis.

Let us first consider the Gnostics. The very meaning of the word Gnostic is to know. The Gnostics were the first philosophers and theologians of the Christian Church; they had an inner esoteric teaching which they claimed came direct from Jesus and the Apostles. These philosophers were not only the most cultured in the Christian ranks, but were zealous workers in their faith; they endeavored to formulate Christianity as a universal philosophy. They lived strictly and followed the path of righteousness, striving by every means to purify themselves and to realize by daily practice the teachings of the Master, seeking always the science of realities--the knowledge of God, hence wisdom was their goal and spiritual things their study. They looked at the problem of cosmogony and anthropogeny from above, and in this they may have been as reasonable in thelr proper domain as the modern scientist who looks at the problem from below. Until the middle of the second century, at least, they continued a part of the General Christian body, but at last the narrowness and bigotry of those who followed the outer tradition succeeded in having them denounced as heretics; and this chiefly for contending that the teachings of Christ contained a wisdom that transcended the comprehension of the multitude.

The Gnostics had their Mysteries and Initiations. Even in the recently discovered "Acts of John" we have a fragrnent of the early Gnostic ritual of the Mysteries; there is also mention of some of the degrees such as the "Initiation of the Cross," and in the "Pistis Sophia," the "Books of the Savior," and the "Book of the Great Logos," there is constant mention of the Mysteries. The Christian Mysteries, like the Eleusinian, were divided into two parts, the Lesser and the Greater.

Beside the Greek original Gnostic works above mentioned, we have some Gnostic fragments recovered from the polemical writings of the Church Fathers, but as these writers were the most bitter opponents of the

Gnostics they are not a very accurate source of information. Iraeneus is our chief informant, but he has been shown to be entirely unreliable.

I am convinced that the Gnostics came the nearest to preserving the Gnosis of the Master, but even with them, after a time, the great spiritual truths became intermixed with many fantastic ideas.

I regret that space does not permit an extended examination of this much neglected field of original Christian mysticism, but as all admit the existence of a Gnostic Gnosis, it will not be necessary to go into further details.

Let us now look at the Orthodox Gnosis. This represents the narrower stream, if not in volume at least in exclusiveness, and though the later Church fathers condemned the followers of this tradition equally with the Gnostics, for some centuries it had a wide following among the more intelligent of the early church.

We will trace this tradition more fully: Polycarp, a fellow disciple with Ignatius and St. John, in his Epistle to the Church at Philippi, writes, "I trust that ye are well versed in the Sacred Scriptures, and that nothing is hid from you, but to me this privilege is not yet granted." (Anti Nicene Fathers, Am. Ed. Vol. I, p. 35.) It is evident from this that there was a hidden teaching in which Polycarp was not yet instructed, for he trusts that those to whom he writes are farther advanced, that there is nothing hid from them, so Polycarp evidently was not yet a full Initiate.

In the Apistle to Barnabas its writer says, "If I should take the trouble to communicate to you some portion of what I have myself received, it would prove to me a sufficient reward that I minister to such spirits." (Epistle to Barnabas, Ch. I.) It is clear from this that Barnabas had received instruction in addition to that possessed by those to whom he wrote.

Ignatius, in his Epistle to the Ephesians, writes, "I know both who I am and to whom I write. . . Ye are initiated into the mysteries of the Gospel with Paul, the holy, the martyred, inasmuch as he was a 'chosen vessel.' " (Ch. XII.) In the Epistle of Ignatius to the Trallians, he says, "For might not I write to you things more full of mystery? But I fear to do so, lest I should inflict injury on you who are but babes.
Pardon me in this respect, lest, as not being able to receive their weighty import, ye should be strangled by them. For even I, though I am bound (for Christ) and am able to understand heavenly things, the angelic orders, and the different sorts of Angels and hosts, the

distinctions between powers and dominions, and the diversities between thrones and authorities, the mightiness of the Aeons, and the preeminence of the cherubim and seraphim, the sublimity of the spirit, the Kingdom of the Lord, and, above all, the incomparable majesty of Almighty God--though I am acquainted with these things, yet I am not therefore by any means perfect; nor am I such a disciple as Paul or Peter." (Ch. V.)

This passage is important as showing that the Mysteries dealt with "heavenly things," the "angelic orders," etc.

In his "Epistle to the Philadelphians" he says, "The priests indeed are good, but the High Priest [Hierophant] is better; to whom the holy of holies has been committed, and who alone has been trusted with the secrets of God." (Ch. IX.)

In the "Constitutions of the Holy Apostles," ascribed to Clement, Bishop of Rome, the author in speaking of the instruction of catechurnens and their initiation says, "Now, after what manner those ought to live that are initiated into Christ. . . has been said in the foregoing directions. But it is reasonable not to leave even those who are not yet initiated without assistance. . . And when it remains that the catechumen is to be baptized, let him learn what concerns the renunciation of the devil, and the joining of himself with Christ; for it is fit that he should first abstain from things contrary, and then be admitted to the Mysteries. He must beforehand purify his heart from all wickedness of disposition, from all spot and wrinkle, and then partake of the holy things....that so the candidate for baptism, when he is anointed, may be free from all ungodliness, and may become worthy of initiation." (Book VII, Sec. III.)

We now come to Clement of Alexandria. He was a disciple of Pantaenus, master of the Cathechetical School in Alexandria and afterward succeeded him as the head of the school in 189 A. D. Clement speaks of Pantaenus and two others, probably Tatian and Theodotus, as "preserving the tradition of the blessed doctrine derived directly from the holy apostles, Peter, James, John and Paul, the sons receiving it from the father, came by God's will to us also to deposit those ancestral and apostolic seeds. . . the Lord. . . allowed us to communicate of those divine Mysteries, and of that holy light, to those who are able to receive them. He did not certainly disclose to the many what did not belong to the many; but to the few to whom he knew that they belonged who were capable of receiving and being moulded according to them. But secret things are entrusted to speech, not to writing, as in the case with God. And if one say that it is

written, 'there is nothing secret which shall not be revealed, nor hidden which shall not be disclosed,' let him also hear from us, that to him who hears secretly, even what is secret shall be manifested. This is what was predicted by this oracle. And to him who is able secretly to observe what is delivered to him, that which is veiled shall be disclosed as truth; and what is hidden to the many, shall appear manifest to the few. For why do not all know the truth ? Why is not righteousness loved, if righteousness belongs to all?

But the Mysteries are delivered mystically, that what is spoken may be in the mouth of the speaker; rather not in his voice, but in his understand-ing.   The

writing of this memoranda of mine, I well know, is weak when com-pared with that spirit, full of grace, which I was privileged to hear. But it will be an image to recall the archetype to him who was struck with the thyrsus [a wand borne by Initiates with which candidates were touched during the ceremony of Initiation]. . . We profess not to explain se-cret things sufficiently--far from it--but only to recall them to memory, whether we have forgot aught, or whether for the purpose of not forget-ting.   Some

things I purposely omit, in the exercise of a wise selection, afraid to write what I guarded against speaking; not grudging--for that were wrong--but fearing for my readers, lest they should stumble by taking them in a wrong sense; and, as the proverb says, we should be found 'reaching a sword to a child.'... some things my treatise will hint; on some it will linger; some it will merely mention. It will try to speak imperceptibly, to exhibit secretly, and to demonstrate silently." (The Stromata, Book I, Ch. I.)

Again in speaking of "The Mysteries of the faith not to be divulged to all," he says, "But since this tradition is not published alone for him who perceives the magnificence of the word; it is requisite, therefore, to hide in a mystery the wisdom spoken, which the Son of God taught. Now, therefore, Isaiah the prophet has his tongue purified by fire, so that he may be able to tell the vision. And we must purify not the tongue alone, but also the ears, if we attempt to be partakers of the truth. Such were the impediments in the way of my writing. And even now I fear, as it is said, 'to cast the pearls before swine, lest they tread them under foot, and turn and rend us.' For it is difficult to exhibit the really pure and transparent words respecting the true light, to swinish and untrained hearers, for scarcely would anything which they could hear be more ludicrous than these to the multitude; nor any subjects, on the other hand, more admirable or more inspiring to those of noble nature. 'But the natural man receiveth not the things of the Spirit of God; for they are foolishness to him.' But the wise do not utter with their mouth what they reason in council. 'But what ye hear in the ear,' says the Lord, 'proclaim upon the

houses' [in the assembly of the Initiates, not to the men in the street]; bidding them receive the secret traditions of the true knowledge, and expound them aloft and conspicuously; and as we have heard in the ear, so to deliver them to whom it is requisite; but not enjoining us to communicate to all without distinction, what is said to them in parables." (The Stromata, Book I, Ch. 12.)

Again, he says, "He who is still blind and dumb, not having understanding, or the undazzled and keen vision of the contemplative soul, which the Savior confers, like the uninitiated at the mysteries, or the unmusical at dances, not being yet pure and worthy of the pure truth but still discordant and disordered and material, must stand outside of the divine choir. 'For we compare spiritual things with spiritual.' Wherefore, in accordance with the method of concealment, the truly sacred Word, truly divine and most necessary for us, deposited in the shrine of truth, was by the Egyptians indicated by what were called among them Adyta, and by the Hebrews by the Veil. Only the consecrated . . . were allowed access to them. For Plato also thought it not lawful for the impure to touch the pure.' Thence the prophecies and oracles are spoken in enigmas, and the mysteries are not exhibited incontinently to all and sundry, but only after certain purifications and previous instructions." (The Stromata, Book V, Ch. IV.)

Clement then takes up the symbolic and allegorical method of writing employed by the philosophers, and quotes many passages from the Scriptures to show that Jesus and the Apostles employed the same method. "The apostle in contradistinction to gnostic perfection," he says, "calls the common faith the foundation and sometimes milk." He speaks of the building as the "gnostic superstructure" or "gnostic edifice" and says, "it was impossible that gifts of this sort could be written without disguise." "But," he continues, "the Gnostic apprehends. Now, then, it is not wished that all things should be exposed indiscriminately to all and sundry, or the benefits of wisdom communicated to those who have not even in a dream been purified in soul (for it is not allowed to hand to every chance comer what has been procured with such laborious efforts); nor are the mysteries of the word to be expounded to the profane." (Stromata, Book V, Ch. IX.)

In the next chapter he says distinctly that "there is an instruction of the perfect. . . to whom God wished to make known what is the riches of the glory of this mystery among the nations. So that on the one hand, then, are the mysteries which were hid till the time of the apostles, and were delivered by them as they received from the Lord and concealed in the Old Testament, were manifested to the saints. And, on the other hand, there is 'the riches of the glory of the

mystery in the Gentiles,' which is faith and hope in Christ; which in another place he has called the 'foundation.' " He says that the "knowledge does ot appertain to all" and quotes Paul to this effect (Col. II, 2, 3). "Blessed be our Lord, Brethren," he says, 'who has put into our hearts wisdom and the understanding of His secrets. . . . It is but for few to comprehend these things. . . Instruction, which reveals hidden things, is called illumination, as it is the teacher only who uncovers the lid of the ark.

....'For I know,' says the Apostle, 'that when I come to you, I shall come in the fullness of the blessing of Christ.'" He then quotes Paul concerning the fullness of the blessing of Christ "designating the spiritual gift, and the gnostic communicatlon, which being present he desires to impart to them present as 'the fullness of Christ, according to the revelation of the mystery sealed in the ages of eternity, but now manifested by the prophetic Scriptures, according to the command of the eternal God.'.. But only to a few of them is shown what those things are which are contained in the mystery. Rightly, then, PIato, in the epistIes, treating of God, says, 'We must speak in enigmas; that should the tablet come, by any mischance on its leaves, either by sea or land, he who reads may remain ignorant.' . Akin to this is what the holy apostle Paul says, preserving the prophetic and truly ancient secret from which the teachings that were good were derived by the Greeks, 'Howbeit we speak wisdom among them who are perfect.' " (Stromata, Book V, Ch. X. )

"Wisdom," he declares, "to be certain knowledge, being a sure and irrefragable apprehension of things divine and human, comprehending the present, past, and future.

. . and it is irrefragable by reason, inasmuch as it has been communicated. . . . And the gnosis itself is that which has descended by transmission to a few, having been imported unwritten by the apostles." (Stromata, Book VI, Ch. VII.)

These quotations might easily be extended, but a sufficient number has been given to show that Clement knew of a secret teaching and was writing for the benefit of those who, like himself, were initiates in the Christian Mysteries. Clement quotes continually from the Scriptures to illustrate the mystic teaching, thus showing that he recognized the passages to which we referred earlier as evidencing the existence of a hidded, esoteric, teaching. The Gnostic was one who knew, an Initiate of the Mysteries.

Let us now turn to Origen, the noted pupil of Clement, and beyond doubt the greatest scholar in the early church. In his famous controversy with Celsus mally references were made to the secret teachings of the church. Celsus charges Christianity with being a secret

system. Origen replying, that while certain things were secret, others were public, says, "But that there should be certain doctrines, not made known to the multitude, which are (revealed) after the exoteric ones have been taught, is not a peculiarity of Christianity alone, but also of philosophic systems, in which certain truths are exoteric and others esoteric. Some of the hearers of Pythagoras were content with his ipse dixit; while others were taught in secret those doctrines which were not deemed fit to be communicated to profane and insufficiently prepared ears. Moreover, all the Mysteries that are celebrated everywhere throughout Greece and barbarous countries, although held in secret, have no discredit thrown upon them, so that it is in vain that he endeavors to calumniate the secret doctrine of Christianity, seeing he does not correctly understand its nature." (Origen Against Celsus, Book I, Ch. VII.)

Again Origen says, "I have not yet spoken of the observance of all that is written in the Gospels, each one of which contains much doctrine difficult to be understood, not merely by tke multitude, but even by certain of the more intelligent, including a very profound explanation of the parables which Jesus delivered to 'those without,' while reserving the exhibition of their full meaning for those who had passed beyond the stage of exoteric teaching, and who came to Him privately in the house. . . what we have said is sufficient by way of answer to the unphilosophic sneers of Celsus, in comparing the inner mysteries of the church of God to the cats and apes, and crocodiles, and goats, and dogs of Egypt." (Origen Against Celsus, Book III, Ch. XXI.)

A little further on in the same Book he again says, "And if you come to the books written after the time of Jesus, you will find that those multitudes of believers who hear the parables are as it were, 'without' and worthy only of exoteric doctrines, while the disciples learn in private the explanation of the parables." (Origen Against Celsus, Book III, Ch. LVI.)

Celsus criticised the Christians for inviting sinners into the Church. He says that in other Mysteries he only is invited who has "clean hands and a prudent tongue; he only who is pure from all pollution and whose soul is conscious of no evil and who has lived well and justly." Origen replies that, "It is not the same to invite those who are sick in soul to be cured, and those who are in health to the knowledge and study of divine things. We, however, keeping both these things in view, at first invite all men to be healed, and exhort those who are sinners to come to the consideration of the doctrines which teach men not to sin, and those who are devoid of understanding to those which beget wisdom, and those who are children to rise

in their thoughts to manhood, and those who are simply unfortunate to good fortune, or-- which is the more appropriate term to use to blessedness. And when those who have been turned toward virtue have made progress, and have shown that they have been purified by the word, and have led as far as they can a better life, then and not before do we invite them to participation in our mysteries. 'For we speak wisdom among them that are perfect.'"? (Origen against Celsus, Book III, Ch. LIX.)

Origen then explains that in the Christian Mysteries as in all others those are received who have "clean hands," who are "athletes in piety and every virtue." "Whoever is pure not only from all defilement," he says, "but from what are regarded as lesser transgressions, let him be boldly initiated in the mysteries of Jesus, which properly are made known only to the holy and the pure. . . He who acts as an initiator, according to the precepts of Jesus, will say to those who have been purified in heart, 'He whose soul has, for a long time, been conscious of no evil, and especially since he yielded himself to the healing of the word, let such a one hear the doctrines which were spoken in private by Jesus to His genuine disciples.' Therefore in the comparison which he institutes between the procedure of the initiators into the Grecian mysteries, and the teachers of the doctrine of Jesus, he does not know the difference between inviting the wicked to be healed, and initiating those already purified into the sacred mysteries ! Not to participation in mysteries, then, and to fellowship in the wisdom hidden in a mystery, which God ordained before the world to the glory of His saints, do we invite the wicked man, and the thief. . . but such as these we invite to be healed. . . Others, again, which to the pure in soul and body exhibit 'the revelation of the mystery, which was kept secret since the world began, but now is made manifest by the Scriptures of the prophets,' and 'by the appearing of our Lord Jesus Christ,' which 'appearing' is manifested to each one of those who are perfect, and which enlightens the reason in the true knowledge of things. . . God the Word was sent, indeed, as a physician to sinners, and also as a teacher of divine mysteries to those who are already pure and who sin no more." ( Origen Against; Celsus, Book III, Ch. LX, LXI, LXII.)

Archilaus, Bishop of Cesarea in Mesopotamia, says, "The Lord spake in parables to those who were incapable of hearing, but to His disciples He explained these parables in private. For the illumination of the glory is for those who have been enlightened, while the blinding is for them who believe not. These mysteries, which the church now declares to you who are transferred from the lists of the catechumens, it is not her custom to declare to the Gentiles. For we do

not declare the mysteries touching the Father, and the Son, and the Holy Spirit to a Gentile; neither do we speak of the mysteries plainly in presence of the catechumens; but many a time we express ourselves in an occult manner, so that the faithful who have intelligence may apprehend the truths referred to, while those who have not that intelligence may receive no hurt." (Anti Nicene Fathers, Vol. VI, p. 235.)

Quotations of this import could be extended, if necessary, but it is now beyond question that there existed in the early church a definite

institution called the "Sacred Mysteries" or the "Mysteries of Jesus,"
wherein was taught a higher wisdom. The church to-day thinks it has
accomplished its mission by producing the saint, and points to the good
man as the crowning glory. Whereas in the early days of the church the
attainment of purity was not the goal, but merely the beginning. There
were three stages or degrees through which men passed--Purification, Illumination, and Perfection. Purification led to saintship; Illumination
gave interior knowledge, the Gnosis taught in the Mysteries; Perfection
was the attainment of unity with the Divine. The early church went on
from the point where the modern church leaves off, and taking the saint
led him to the Beatific Vision.

During these early centuries there was a struggle between the two elements in Christianity--the few who possessed the inner teaching, and
the mass of common believers. The exoteric element finally gained su-
premacy, and the Mystics were denounced as heretics. The Mysteries, as
an organized institution, ceased temporarily for lack of suitable material. The Sublime Secret, however, was not lost, for the light continued
to burn through all the ages.

From time to time efforts were made to revive the institution to its for-
rner glory, but the conditions of the age were too gross and supersti-
tious. "Two streams may nevertheless be tracked through Christendom,
streams which had as their source the vanished Mysteries. One was the
stream of mystic learning, flowing from the Wisdom, the Gnosis, imparted in the Mysteries [both Pagan and Christian]; the other was the
stream of mystic contemplation, equally part of the Gnosis, leading to
the ecstasy, to spiritual vision.

This latter, however, diverted from knowledge, rarely

attained the true ecstacies." (Esoteric Christianity, p. 107.)

These two streams can be traced through the Gnostic Schools of Syria
and Egypt, the Manichaeans, Paulicians, Albigenses, Cathari, Templars,
The Knights of Malta, Troubadours, Lollards, Rosicrucians, Alchemists, Hermetic Masters, and many other mystic orders.

Thus the Secret Teaching has been passed along down the ages. Scholars, Saints and Martyrs have everywhere sought the hidden truth, and the various occult brotherhoods, mystical associations, and many so-called heretical sects, have been links in the chain of that Wisdom Religion, which is the source of all religious schools and philosophies. The great Spiritual Hierarchy, the guardian of the mystic tradition (which constitutes the science of the soul), has always been and always will be as ready to give, as man in his evolutionary condition is ready to receive, instruction in Divine Wisdom.

With the growth of the race old forms perished, and those who identified the spirit with the form thought all was destroyed. But as the form perished the conscious life sought new embodiment, and thus have the guardians of truth passed along the higher knowledge to these who were ready to receive it. Who then can doubt a definite design in the preservation of the Divine Truth through all the ages?

We shall now turn to Freemasonry and show that this institution is a vehicle of the same occult knowledge; that the Ancient Wisdom is still embodied in its symbolism and rites and is obtainable as it always has been, by those who possess the key. In showing this connection and possession we will consider more fully the meaning of Initiation in the Pagan and Christian Mysteries, to which I invite your attention in the following

## 7

## LECTURE VI

**T**HE MEANING OF TRUE INITIATION.
It is a well known fact that the biographies of all the great World-Saviors closely resemble each other. All are represented as divinely begotten, and born at the same time of the year, all are threatened with death in infancy; all are tempted, persecuted, and finally slain; all descend into hell and after three days rise from the dead; and at last all ascend into heaven and become glorified Gods.

What is the explanation of this wonderful similarity in the lives of Jesus, Apollonius, Mithra, Buddha, Krishna, Zoroaster, etc.? The solution of this remarkable identity is to be found in the fact that all these Saviors were Initiates into the Mysteries of Antiquity. The various narratives do not describe the physical life of the heroes, but the inner mystic life, being but a materialization of the mystic life of the Initiate. The physical plane biographies might greatly vary, but their lives as Initiates are ever the same.

In our study of the meaning of true Initiation we shall see the origin of these stories. I will commence at the beginning and trace the various stages of progress.

In the first place, a man to be recognized as a candidate, must be pure and holy, and possess a well developed and well-trained mind. Having attained the exoteric "good life," he enters on the preparation for Initiation. Certain conditions have now to be fulfilled and certain attributes acquired. The aspirant for Initiation must be "worthy and well qualified, duly and truly prepared." During this period the candidate is said to be treading the Probationary Path, the Path which leads up to the "Strait Gate," beyond which is the "Narrow Way," or the "Path of Holiness," the "Way of the Cross," which leadeth unto life.

Let me briefly sum up the attributes to be acquired:

1.    Discrimination. This means that the aspirant becomes able to distinguish between the Eternal and the Temporal, the Real and the Unreal, so that what is unreal to the world becomes real to him. He must set his affections on things above, loosen the ties on worldly objects, and fix his aspirations on things pertaining to the unseen. This has been called "allegiance to the Higher Self."

2.    Devotion to Right. The aspirant here learns to do what is right because it is right, without regard to his own gain or loss. This is sometimes called indifference to personal reward as the fruit of good actions. This indifference is the natural result of the previous step, men cease to crave for earthly rewards when they realize their impermanent character.

3.    The six qualifications (a) Control of Thoughts-- purity and calmness which result from control of the mind. (b) Control of Actions--mastery of one's actions and words. (c) Tolerance--freedom from bigotry, from an exaggerated attachment to any doctrinal belief, leading to a wide impartiality. (d) Forbearance--freedom from resentment in respect to real or fancied wrongs. (e) Steadfastness--incapability of being turned aside from one's purpose. (f) Faith - confidence in the power of the Master to teach the truth, and of one's self to grasp and wield it.

4.    Direct Order or Succession--a clearly defined desire for spiritual existence, and union with the higher ideals.

5.    Readiness for Initiation--the result of the previous acquirements. The candidate is not expected to fully develop these attributes, he must, however, have made progress in

them before he is ready for the first step on the Path Proper.

When the time comes that he is regarded fit for Initiation, he is conducted by the Master, who has been watching over his earlier progress, to the threshold where the "Guardians of the Mysteries" open for him the "Strait Gate."

The Path Proper is divided into four stages, or five stages with the culmination. In the first four stages -
-the period between the good man and the triumphant Master--the neophyte is to cast off the ten fetters that bind him to the circle of rebirth, and which keep him from realizing Nirvana--the highest state of spiritual consciousness. No partial success will here suffice, he must be entirely free before he can pass from one stage to the next. When these fetters are cast off the ego is ready for the fifth stage--full adeptship. He becomes an "Asekha" Adept--a Christ Triumphant. The first step in the Hindu system is called Sotapatti or Sohan. One who attains this level is called the Sotapanna or Sowani--he who has entered the stream, one who has begun the higher human evolution. This evolution is that of the Divine Child, and is called in different systems by different names Christ, Horus, Buddha, etc.

It was at this first great Initiation that the Divine Child was born in man. This was spoken of as the "New" or "Second Birth"--a mystic term often employed to denote the rites of Initiation. In India, even to-day, the higher castes are called the "twice born," and the ceremony that makes them such is called Initiation. The rite of baptism is connected with the first Initiation. It is a symbol of purification, and signifies that the candidate has attained the purity of character necessary for acceptance. "In all these Mysteries," says Dr. Mackey, "the first step taken by the candidate was a lustration or purification. The aspirant was not permitted to enter the sacred vestibule, or take any part in the secret formula of Initiation, until, by water or by fire, he was emblematically purified from the corruptions of the world which he was about to leave behind." (Symbolism of Freemasonry, Mackey, p. 93.) The purification of the body was symbolic of a purification of the heart.

Frederic Portal, in speaking of the Egyptian Mysteries, says, "In Egyptian Cosmogony. . . water was the mother of the world, the matrix of all created beings. Man was considered as an image of the world, the Initiate was to be born again to a new life and the baptism thenceforward symbolized the primeval waters; it was on this account that the Initiate was called "Moses," a word signifying in Egyptian, according to Josephus, saved from the water, or by the water. . . water was a

symbol of purity and designated the birth of the pure or Initiated." (A Comparison of Egyptian Symbols with those of the Hebrews, p. 81.) Again, he says, speaking of the method of Egyptian baptism, "Horus and

Thoth-Lunus pour water on the head of the candidate, who is transformed to divine life and to purity." The legend accompanying this scene he translates thus, "Horus, son of Isis, baptises with water and fire." This is repeated three times. The name given to the baptized or anointed, as we have seen, was Moses, signifying regenerated, or begotten again. Remember the lawgiver of the - Jews was called by the Egyptians Moses--one saved by water, or, in other words, one Initiated. In the Acts of the Apostles we are told that Moses was learned in all the wisdom of the Egyptians; if so, he must have been an Initiate. The great Mystery of Egypt was this second birth, the Birth of Horus.

Says W. Marsham Adams, "Throughout the sacred writings of Egypt, there is no doctrine of which more frequent mention is made than that of a divine birth." (The Egyptian Doctrine of Light, Adams, p. 89.)

The candidate was initiated from the Sacred Roll, called the "Book of the Greatest Mysteries," and after passing the Passage of the Sun, the crown of Illumination was placed upon his head. And now the new twice-born, "clothed in power and crowned with light, traverses the abodes or scenes of his former weakness, there to discern, by his own enlightened perception, how it is 'Osiris who satisfies the balance of Him who rules the Heavens; to exert in its supernal freedom his creative will, now the Lord, not the slave of the senses; and to rejoice in the just suffering which wrought his Illumination and Mastery." (Ibid, p. 185.) Hermes in the "Secret Serrnon on the Mountain," discourses on the secret of the New Birth. This might well be called the "Initiation of Tat." - The sermon is in the form of a dialogue between Hermes the Master and Tat the pupil. Tat says, "In the General Sermons, father [a technical name of the Master or Initiator], thou didst speak in riddles most unclear, conversing on Divinity; and when thou saidst no man could e'er be saved before Rebirth, thy meaning thou didst hide.

Further, when I became thy Suppliant, in Wending up the Mount, after thou hadst conversed with me, and when I longed to learn the Sermon (Logos) on Rebirth, (for this beyond all other things is just the thing I know not), thou saidst, that thou wouldst give it me--'when thou shalt have become a stranger to the world.' Wherefore I got me ready and made the thought in me a stranger to the world-illusion."

G.R.S. Mead, in his "Thrice Greatest Hermes," in commenting upon this discourse, says, "The time has come for Tat to receive, through his Master, the touch of the true Mind in Consciousness, the Christ is to be

born in his heart, the light of the Pleroma is to shine in his inmost being. . It is to be a New Birth, a Regeneration, or Rebirth, in the sense of being born from Above." (Thrice Greatest Hermes, Mead, Vol. II, p. 239.) Tat had made himself ready for this Rebirth by passing through three stages of probation. He had been prepared by "Wending up the Mount." The phrase "On the Mountain" or "Wending up the Mountain" is symbolical of the grades of Initiation. The term is of frequent occurence in the Christian Gnostic and Apochryphal writings, and everywhere signifies the "Mount of Initiation." In the popular beliefs, the mountain is called the "Mount of Galilee," on which all the rites of Initiation were performed. But the real "Mount" was no physical elevation, it was the "height of contemplation, an inner state of spiritual consciousness." Tat had been wending his way up this "Mount" and was now ready for the New Birth, "The crowning mystery of the Spiritual Way for all the mystic schools of the time."

"The secret that Tat would learn is the Mystery of the birth from the Virgin Womb - the Birth of Man, the Great Mystery of Regeneration." (Ibid, p. 240.) Tat entreats Hermes to explain to him the manner of this Rebirth. But Hermes cannot tell to Tat the secret in words. It must be self-perceived. "This race my child," says Hermes, "was never taught." This is the "Race" referred to by Philo as the "Race of Devotees who are ever taught more and more to see, let them strive for the Initiation of That-which-is; let them transcend the sun which men perceive [and gaze upon the Light beyond, the True Sun or Logos,] nor ever leave this rank which leads to Perfect Blessedness. Now they who betake themselves to the [Divine] Service [do so], not because of any custom or on someone's advice or appeal, but carried away with Heavenly Love, like those Initiated into the Bacchic and the Corybantic Mysteries; they are afire with God until they behold the object of their love." Again Philo says, "Now this natural class of men [lit. race] is to be found in many parts of the inhabited world; for both the Grecian and non-Grecian world must needs share in the perfect Good." (Philo on The Contemplative Life.) This "Race," then, was the Race of Initiates, the "Race of Elxai" mentioned by Epiphanius. Those attaining this state apprehended the mystery of Rebirth.

Although this spiritual state could not be taught to the neophyte in words, still, as Mead puts it, Hermes can guide Tat toward the realization of the Blessed Sight, by putting himself into the sublime state of consciousness, that Tat, so to speak, bathes, or is baptized in his Master's spiritual presence--the Cup of the Mind. This is the true laying on of hands. Hermes describes the change that takes place in himself when

he passes into the high spiritual consciousness. "Whene'er I see within myself the Simple Vision. . . I have passed through myself into a Body that can never die. And now I am not what I was before; but I am born in Mind." The Master focusses his consciousness in the higher part of his spiritual nature--transfers it to a spiritual vehicle. "The way to do this is not taught, and it cannot be seen by the compound element by means of which thou seest," that is, it cannot be understood from any sensible experience. No physical sight can penetrate this Mystery. "Thou seest me with eyes, my son," says Hermes, "but what I am thou dost not understand." The outer physical forrn of the Master was there. but his soul had been liberated from the body.

This mystery couId only be understood by one who
himself had reached the higher state.

Tat's spiritual senses are being born by the aid of the Master. He says, "Into fierce frenzy and mind fury hast thou plunged me, father, for now no longer do I see myself." He is losing touch with the physical plane consciousness, but that is not enough. Hermes says, "I would, my son, that thou had'st e'en passed right through thyself," that is, passed into the higher vehicle, "the body that can never die." This is the mystery that Hermes could not explain in words. (The Secret Sermon on the Mountain.)

Isis is not permitted to declare the secret of Rebirth openly to Horus. She says, "I may not tell the story of this birth; for it is not permitted to declare the origin of thy descent, O Horus, son of mighty power, Iest afterward the Way-of-Birth of the immortal Gods should be known unto men." (Quoted in Thrice Greatest Hermes, Vol. II, p. 242.) In the Isis mystery tradition we find that it was a part of the work to bestow this higher consciousness. Diodorus informs us that it was Isis who "discovered the Philtre of immortality, by means of which, when her son Horus, who had been plotted against by the Titans, and found dead beneath the waters, not only raised him to life, but also made him a sharer in immortality." Initiation bestowed or restored to the soul the consciousness of immortality. This was truly a new birth, an inner change, a "striking of a new keynote." He who, is reborn into the Gnosis, passes from man into the state of super-man.

The very essence of Gnosis is the fact that man can transcend his present limitations, and become consciously divine. This is true illumination. Those who attained this Hermes or Horus state were to keep silent concerning their powers, and not boast of their Gnosis.

We find this same teaching in the Christian Mysteries. Jesus says, "Except a man be born again he cannot see the Kingdom of God." (John, III, 3.) Peter says, "Seeing ye have purified your souls in obeying the

truth. . . being born again not of corruptible seed but of incorruptible, by the word of God which liveth and abideth forever." (I. Peter I. 22-23.) The birth is spoken of as that of "water and the spirit." in the Mysteries of Jesus, as in all others, baptism was always connected with the first Initiatory Rite. Many illustrations of this pivot doctrine of the early church might be cited from Gnostic writings. The over-writer of the Naassene Document tells us that the Lesser Mysteries pertain to fleshly-generation, whereas the Greater, deal with the new or second birth, with regeneration and not with genesis. In speaking of the Mystery of Re-generation, the writer says, "For this is the Gate of Heaven, and this is the House of God, where the Good God dwells alone; into which [house] no impure [man] shall come--no psychic, no fleshly [man]-- but it is kept under watch for the spiritual alone-- where, when they come, they must cast away their garments, and all become bridegrooms, ob-taining their true manhood through the Virginal Spirit. For this is the Virgin, big with Child, conceiving and bearing a son--not psychic, not fleshly, but a blessed Aeon of Aeons," that is, an immortal God. This is the birth of the Christ, or Horus in man, the Great Mystery that awaits us when we have made ourselves strangers to the world illusion, as Hermes puts it, or as Jesus says in one of his new found sayings, "Except ye fast to the world, ye shall in no wise find the Kingdom of God." This writing is important, as it shows that the inner teaching of Christianity was identical with the tenets of the other Mysteries--Eleusinian, Egypt-ian, Mithraic, Dionysian, etc. The date of this Christian over-writer was about the middle of the second century.

In the mystery ritual of Initiation in the "Acts of John," we read, "Who I am, thou shalt know when I depart [that is, by contrast]. What I am seen to be, that am I not; but what I am, thou shalt see when thou comest." In other words, this spiritual state must be realized to be known, and only those who had attained the Christ state--the Perfect Initiate-- could know it.

-Remember the words of Hermes already cited, "Thou seest me with eyes, my son; but what I am thou dost not understand." This consciousness transcends man's normal state.

Although the new birth primarily signfied the first great Initiation, when the white robed neophyte entered the "Communion of Saints," still, the mystic term might well indicate the other stages of soul development, for it signalized the entrance to a new life. The Initiate is ushered into a new state of consciousness at each stage, as much so as the new born infant when ushered into physical existence. It is difficult for us to imagine these higher states of consciousness, but each

state ushered the candidate into a new realm, where, while retaining hold on the physical plane, he had to adapt himself to new conditions. Each rite was a sign and symbol of spiritual consciousness which had come to the new born disciple. "The Christ principle, the intuitional Wisdom, is born in the soul, and when that Buddhic [spiritual] consciousness is awakened, the soul becomes again, as it were, a little child, born into that higher life of the Initiated, which is in truth the Kingdom of Heaven." (Christian Creed, Leadbeater, p. 76.) The new born Son, the "little child," a technical term denoting one just Initiated, is now to live the divine life and become "like unto the Father"--pass from Sonship to Perfection.

The new or spiritual birth, then, is a mystic fact. The materialization of this inner truth into the dogma of the "Virgin Birth" must have been a comparatively late development in the evolution of popular or general Christianity. The dogma is not to be found in the common document, and the earlier traditions all state that Joseph was the natural father of Jesus. Celsus accused the Christians of changing their gospel story many times in order to better answer the objections of opponents. This is true only of the exoteric tradition.

Now let us consider the various stages in the evolution of the Christ in man. To understand this higher evolution, which constituted the work of the True Mysteries, we must understand man's constitution.

We will use here the Christian terminology because of familiarity with the terms, but the facts described are the same in all systems.

Christian theology usually accepts the three-fold division--Spirit, Soul and Body. This is sound, but in order to understand the Mystery of the life of the Divine Child, especially his crucifixion, resurrection and ascension, we shall need a further subdivision of man's constitution. The spirit is itself a trinity, containing the three aspects of the divine life-- Intelligence, Love and Will; the soul is twofold, composed of the mind and emotional nature; the body is the material instrument of the soul and spirit, and is also dual, being composed of the dense physical body and its etheric double. These lower portions or principles--the dual physical body, the desire or emotional body, and the mental body--form the natural body spoken of by of St. Paul. The Apostle says, "There is a natural body and there is a spiritual body." The spiritual is made up of the three higher principles.

The lowest of these is sometimes called the Causal body, the second division the Bliss or Glorified or resurrected body, the third and highest division, the Atmic body.

These principles or bodies are correlated with the lower five of the seven planes of our universe. The normal evolution of mankind takes place on the three lowest planes; the Super-normal evolution, that of the Initiate, proceeds on the next two planes which are the spiritual. These five planes constitute the field of the evolution of consciousness until the "human merges into the divine."

Bearing these divisions of man's constitution in mind and the planes to which they are correlated, we are ready to study the mystery of the Christ evolution.

This evolution is set forth in the story of the Mystic Christ. The Mystic Christ is one aspect of the Christ of the Mysteries. The Mystic Christ deals with this Christ evolution, which is the development of the Love, or second aspect, of the unfolding divine spirit in man, called the Christ; the other aspect, called the Mythic Christ, is the Logos, the second Aspect or Person of the Trinity, descending into matter.

The development of the first division of the spiritual body, the aspect of intelligence, takes place in the ordinary life of the world. When this intellectual development has - been carried to a high point, accompanied by moral development, then the man is ready for the evolution of the second aspect of the spirit, the second division of the spiritual body, that of Love, called the Christ.

We will consider first this aspect of the Mystic Christ--the evolution of the Christ of the human spirit. This is the "Christ who is in every one of us, who is born and lives, is crucified, rises from the dead, and ascends into heaven in every suffering and

triumphant Son of Man." This is the story of the mystic life of every Initiate.

We have seen that at the first great Initiation the Christ is born in the disciple. This is the second birth to which we have referred. He is born into the Kingdom of Heaven as a little child--the name given to a new Initiate. Jesus said that except a man becomes as a little child he cannot enter the Kingdom.

Every such child is beset by perils that do not befall others. The dark powers seek his undoing, but the Christ child once born cannot be destroyed. He grows in wisdom and spiritual stature until the time comes for the second great Initiation, symbolized by the baptism "by water and the spirit," which confers on him the powers necessary for the Teacher. He then goes forth into the world to labor, and is led by the Spirit into the wildnerness, and is there exposed to severe temptations. The evil powers strive to lure him from his set purpose, bidding him use his unfolding powers to secure worldly ends. But triumphant over those

temptations, he uses the powers which he would not employ for his own needs, to save the world. This devotion to service leads him to the third great Initiation, symbolized by the Transfiguration. He again ascends "the mountain apart," the sacred mount of initiation, but he cannot there remain. He sets his face resolutely toward Jerusalem, where he is to meet the baptism of the Holy Ghost and of Fire--the final test and the last stage of the "Way of the Cross." He is now ready for the fourth great Initiation, symbolized by the passion. He has become victorious over the lower nature, and is willing, to nail it to the cross. Although he enters into Jerusalem in triumph and in full confidence that he is prepared for the sacrifice, there comes the bitter agony in the garden, and for a moment he prays that the cup may pass--that bitter cup of betrayal, desertion and pain, when in the horrors and darkness of this final trial it seems that even the Father has forsaken him. His inner vision is blinded, and he thinks himself alone; but he is still steadfast, and with an unconquering trust he yields up the lower life, and descends into hell, that no region in the universe may remain untrodden. But liberated from the material body he sees the light once more, and feels himself again as the Son, and is ready for the fifth Initation, symbolized by the resurrection and ascension, and rises triumphant over death and hell; then He remains for a time on earth to teach his disciples, and at last ascends into Heaven.

This story of the gospel biography sets forth in allegory the life history of every Initiate. The initiatory rites symbolize the states through which the candidate passes. The stage of the soul's progress typified by death, burial and resurrection, was called in Egypt "the death rite," and by the Gnostic Christians "the Initiation of the Cross."

The candidate was received by the initiating Hierophant at the proper time and place, usually a secluded chamber in a temple or pyramid, and laid on the stone floor with arms outstretched; sometimes on a wooden cross, which was hollowed out to support the human figure. He was then touched with the thyrsus, the "spear of the crucifixion," on the heart; he then passed into a deep trance. The body was placed in a sarcopnagus of stone, a vault or tomb beneath the floor of the Hall of Initiation, and carefully guarded.

Meantime, while the body was dead and buried, he himself was fully alive in the invisible world (Hades), and undergoing what was called the tests of earth, water, fire and air. He then put on his perfected Bliss Body, which was now fully organized as a vehicle of consciousness: After the third day the cross, bearing the body, was lifted up and carried out into the air on the east side of the pyramid or temple and placed on a sloping surface ready to greet the rising sun. At the

moment the first rays touched the face, the perfected Initiate, the Horus or Christ, rose from the dead, resuscltated the body, and glorified it by his resurrected body, no longer a natural man but a spiritual man, having overcome death and hell.

The trance typifies his "death unto sin"; the revival, his "rebirth or resurrection unto righteousness." In the "Acts of John" there is preserved the tradition of the inner schools on the mystery of the "Initiation of the Cross." We find here no trace of the literal historic tradition. The crucifixion was an inner experience of the soul. The cross was a symbol of the crucifixion of the soul in the matter and its regeneraton. "Mystical death," says Dr. Hartman, "is identical with spiral regeneration." ("Magic White and Black," Hartman, p. 185.) The cross also symbolizes cosmic processes. If the "Acts of John" had given the drama of Initiation, as well as the liturgy, we should undoubtedly have seen that the passion of Christ was something quite different from what has been popularly supposed. I have shown in the preceding lectures that the symbolic rites of "crucifixion" and the "resurrection of the dead," were connected with the most world-wide mystic festivals of antiquity, a highly important fact, for it enables us to understand the meaning of the Christian crucifixion and resurrection.

When the neophyte reached a certain stage of perfection or enlightenment, he was said to "rise from the dead." The phrase "resurrection from the dead" is a mystical phrase used to represent the new birth or resurrection, the Gnostic illumination. When the candidate reached this stage he was immortal--had attained unbroken consciousness of his spiritual ego; he became now the triumphant Christ, "I am he that liveth and was dead; and behold, I am alive forevermore, Amen; and have the keys of hell and death." (Rev. I, 18.)

Let me here cite several authorities regarding this important ceremony: Dr. Oliver, speaking of Initiation, says, "It was considered to be a mystical death or oblivion of all the stains and imperfections of a corrupted and evil life, as well as a descent into hell, where every pollution was purged by lustrations of fire and water; and the perfect Epopt was then said to be regenerated or new born, restored to a renovated existence of life, light and purity, and placed under divine protection." (History of Initiation, Oliver, p. II.) In his "Signs and Symbols," he again says, "In all the Ancient Mysteries, before an aspirant could claim to participate in the higher secrets of the institution, he was placed within the Pastos, or Bed, or Coffin; or, in other words, was subjected to a solitary confinement for a prescribed period of time, that he might reflect seriously, in seclusion and darkness, on what he was about to undertake. This

was the symboical death of the mysteries, and his deliverance from confinement was the act of regeneration or being born again; or, as it was also termed, being raised from the dead. . . The ceremony here alluded to was, doubtless, the same as the descent into Hades. . . His resurrection from the bed [or tomb] was his restoration to life, - or his regeneration into a new world; and it was virtually the same as his return from Hades. . . The candidate was made to undergo these changes in scenic representation; and was placed under the Pastos in perfect darkness, generally for the space of three days and nights." (Signs and Symbols, Oliver, p. 78).

Dr. Mackey says, "The vault was, in the Ancient Mysteries, symbolic of the grave, for Initiation was symbolic of death, where alone divine Truth is to be found." (Encyclopedia of Freemasonry, Mackey, p. 852.) He again says, "The intention of the ceremonies of Initiation into them, was, by a scenic representation of death, and subsequent restoration to life, to impress the great truths of the resurrection of the dead and the immortality of the soul. . .They were all funereal in their character; they began in sorrow and lamentation, they ended in joy; there was an aphanism, or burial, a pastos, or grave; an euresis, or discovery of what had been lost; and a legend, or mythical reIation--all of which were entirely and profoundly symbolical in their character." (The Symbolism of Freemasonry, Mackey, p. 38).

Faber says, "The Initiation into the Mysteries scenically represented the mystic descent into Hades and the return from thence to the light of day." ("Origin of Pagan Idolatry," Faber, Vol. IV., p. 384)

Many other authorities might be cited in evidence of this ceremony, but this will suffice to prove the ceremony universal and connected with all the Mystery Institutions.

The saying of Jesus that the "Son of Man shall remain three days and three nights in the heart of the earth," corresponds with the ancient rite, but in the gospel story of the resurrection the interval from Friday evening to Sunday morning cannot be regarded as three days and three nights. It has been suggested that the shortening of the time was due to the fact that in the degeneracy of the Mysteries, where attempts were made to minimize all requirements, the original period becarne so tedious to candidates who could not pass into the trance, that the time was reduced from

seventy-two hours to twenty-seven, by just reversing

the figures, thus saving the candidate nearly two full days of solitary confinement. The materialized gospel story, evidently followed this later practice.


These great rites stood originally for great spiritual truths. The body with which the candidate "rose from the dead" was the Bliss Body--the body of the Christ which had been developed during the period of service on earth. This body belongs to the life of the Initiate--the Christ life. Its building begins at the second birth, when the Christ is born in man, and

reaches its completion at the resurrection. During this evolutionary period, when the Son is "being made perfect" the Initiate is called the "Son of Man;" the perfected, risen, and glorified Christ is called the "Son of God."

There is still another feature of the Christ story-- the Ascension. This has to do with the third part of the spiritual body, the putting on of the Atmic body, or the Vesture or Robe of Glory, as it is called in the Pistis Sophia. Spiritual evolution consists in the organization and vitalization of the various Garments or Sheaths of man into Vestures or Robes of Power and Glory, for the use of the Regenerate in the "Path of Ascent," the "Way Above." The highest Vesture prepares the Son for union with the Father, and as a spiritual fact this is symbolized by the Ascension. The material story of the Ascension is an historicization of this inner mystic truth, experienced by every soul that becomes consciously one with God.

"The ascension for humanity is when the whole race has attained the Christ condition, the state of the Son, and that Son becomes one with the Father, and God is all in all. That is the goal, prefigured in the triumph of the Initiate, but reached only when the human race is perfected and when 'the great orphan, Humanity,' is no longer an orphan, but consciously recognizes itself as the Son of God." (Esoteric Christianity, Besant, p. 249.)

8 |

## LECTURE VII

THE MEANING OF TRUE INITIATION.
(Concluded.)

We have seen in the preceding lecture that the Christ of the Mysteries has two aspects--the Mystic and the Mythic. In the Mystic, the Microcosm, Man, the Christ of the Mysteries, represents the second aspect of the divine spirit in humanity, called the Christ; in the Mythic, the Macrocosm, the Cosmos, the Christ of the Mysteries, represents the Logos in His manifestation through His Second Aspect.

In the preceding lecture we have studied the Mystic Christ; now we are to consider the Mythic Christ.

The great facts of the spiritual life were carefully guarded in the Mysteries, and given out to the world only in symbolic language. The Solar or Sun-Myth is the popular teaching concerning the Cosmic Mythic Christ-- the Christ of the Solar Myths or legends. A Myth we must remember is not mere fiction; it may be truer than written history; it is a great truth embodied in a pictorial form. All symbols were employed by Initiates with a definite meaning; we need, therefore, to know the true meaning of the symbols in order to read the true meaning of the Myth. The Solar-Myth sets forth, primarily, the activity of the Logos (the Mythic Christ) in the universe; secondarily, the mystic life of the Initiate. This story of the Sun-God, then, is of utmost importance. It begins with his birth at the winter solstice, after the shortest day of the year, in the early morning hours of Dec. 25th, as the sign Virgo is rising above

| 97 |

the horizon. He is thus born of a Virgin who remains such after giving birth to her Sun-Child, for the celestial Virgo is still unchanged. In the ancient drawings Virgo of the Zodiac is represented as a woman suckling a child; here we find the origin of the symbol of the Madonna.

The Sun-God is weak and feeble in his infancy-- born at the period when the days are shortest and the nights longest, as with-us on this side of the equatorial line. He is beset by perils in his early youth, but he outlives the threatening dangers of darkness and storm, and grows to manhood. However, he is rapidly approaching his crucifixion, and the glorious days preceding the spring equinox are soon to be clouded by the solar disturbances incident upon his crossing the line. This crossing was called the crucifixion, the date varying with each year. But like all so-called death it is an illusion--merely a transition to a higher life. The Sun-God soon rises triurnphantly and ascends into heaven - the storms are dissipated and darkness gives way to all-conquering light. Jupiter, Osiris, Ormuzd, Apollo, are victorious over all their foes. All nature rejoices, celebrating their conquest, and order is re-established in place of the dire confusion that reigned while gloomy Typhon or Ahriman was dominant. Thus everywhere we find the fable that typifies the triumph of Light over darkness. The Sun could not be kept entombed by the elements. He rose from the dead and ascended into heaven, where, at the Summer Solstice, he attained the acme of his glory and perfection. There he rules triumphant and gives his very lite to ripen the fruit and grain and so sustain his worshipers.

These are the salient points in the lives of all the Sun-Gods, for each is born on the 25th of December, and crucified at the Vernal equinox. The birth-date is

fixed, while the death-date is variable. This of itself should be sufficient to show us that both Christmas and Easter (the Sunday following the next full moon after the vernal equinox) were originally solar festivals. A festival calculated by the relative positions of sun and moon, was not designed to commemorate the anniversary of any historical event. We are not here dealing with the history of a man, but with the Hero of a solar myth.

It is interesting to note that the fast preceding the Easter festival is world-wide, and in many countries extended to the time limit of our modern Lent-- forty days. Of course, the original period was only the time intervening between the death and resurrection.

Another interesting fact in this connection is that the animal adopted as the symbol of the Hero is the sign of the Zodiac in which the Sun is at the vernal equinox of his age, and this varies with the precession of the equinoxes. Thus Oannes and Jesus had the sign Pisces-- the Fishes; Mithra and Osiris Taurus--the Bull;
Jupiter-Ammon Aries--the Lamb, etc., while Jesus is also represented as the Lamb.

The Sun-Myth, then, primarily sets forth the activity of the Logos in the Cosmos. This activity is reflected in a partial way in the yearly course of the Sun. The Logos, in His Second Aspect, as the Cosmic-Mythic Christ, descends into matter--becomes incarnate, clothed in "flesh." He thus sacrifices himself by putting on the limitations of matter, entering the womb of matter which is yet virgin, unproductive. This matter has been vivified by the Holy Spirit that it might presently take form and is thus prepared to receive the life of the Second Logos, the Son aspect of God, who took this matter as a vehicle for his energies. The original of the Nicene Creed ran thus, "And was incarnate of the Holy Ghost and the Virgin Mary"--not of the virgin-matter alone, but of matter already pulsating with the life of the Third Logos, so that both the life and the matter surrounded Him as a vesture.

Thus was the descent of the Logos into matter described, in the historicized life of the Saviors, as the "Virgin Birth," and in the Solar Myth as the birth of the Sun-God. The misapprehension of this allegorical illustration, as the life history of a physical human being, and its identification with Jesus, and the various other World-Saviors, was most unfortunate and misleading.

After the incarntaion "come the early workings of the Logos in matter, aptly typified by the infancy of the Myth. To all the feebleness of infancy His Majestic powers bow themselves, letting but little play forth on

the tender forms they ensoul. Matter imprisons, seems as though threatening to slay, its infant King, whose glory is veiled by the limitations He has assumed.
Slowly He shapes it towards high ends, and lifts it into manhood, and then stretches Himself on the cross of matter that He may pour forth from that cross all the powers of His surrendered life. . . Dead He seems and buried out of sight, but He rises again clothed in the very matter in which He seemed to perish, and carries up His body of now radiant matter into heaven, where it receives the downpouring life of the Father, and becomes the vehicle of man's immortal life. For it is the life of the Logos which forms the garment of the soul in man, and He lives it that men may live through the ages and grow to the measure of his own statue. - Truly are we clothed in Him, first materially and then spiritually." (Esoteric Christianity, p. 181.)
The Logos thus leaves the plane of Infinitude, where He is one with the Father, and becomes incarnate, and is finally crucified in space. This is the crucifixion of Christ, the great cosmic sacrifice, represented by the symbol of the crucified Man, which at last becomes materialized into an actual death by crucifixon. The story thus historicized became attached to the various World-Saviors. But the original crucifixion was no disgrace, for the symbol used to represent this mystery is that of the Heavenly Man, with arms outstretched, pouring life and light into His creatures. The
Solar-Myth outlines these great spiritual facts regarding the working of God in the universe.
Every symbol has both a primary and a secondary meaning. The Sun is a symbol of the Logos in its primary meaning, but it also represents any one who is representative of the Logos. Thus a Great Initiate, sent on a

special mission to the world, would, by virtue of his office and mission, have the Sun as his symbol. All who are thus signified would have certain characteristics in common and pass through certain activities, and thus of necessity there would arise similarities in the lives of these ambassadors - their life history as Initiates being outlined by the course of the Sun.

When one becomes an Initiate, or when an Initiate is sent out into the world as a Teacher of men, and especially when a spirit such as Jesus becomes a Hierophant in the Mysteries, then the legends of the Mythic Christ, which have been told of other Great Ones, surround Him and He becomes clothed in the drapery of the Solar-Myth. This is perfectly natural and proper, for the Solar-Myth typifies the various stages of progress through whch He has passed, and this symbolism could only be applied to one who had attained the Christ stage of evolution. With such a one the festival of his nativity became the date when the Son

was born in the Virgin, and the sign of the zodiac at the vernal equinox became that of his crucifixion.

Although these dates were purely arbitrary, adopted from the Sun-Myth, the facts symbolized by the birth, death, and resurrection were living realities in the Mystic life of every Son of God. The adoption of these dates into the materialized lifestory of the Great Saviors is thus readily explained-- they were derived from the solar symbolism. The fact that the rites of Initiation and the Solar-Myth both symbolize the same thing, the former primanly typifying the growth of the soul, secondarily the work of the Logos, and vice versa, made the inter-weaving of the symbolism in this particular perfectly natural, especially so as the great solar festivals, the solstices and equinoxes, were the times when the Mysteries were celebrated and the rites - of Initiation administered. Thus both the Mythic and Mystic Christhave contributed to the gospel story. These Sun-Myth stories have recurred through all the ages, having been told and retold in turn of each great Teacher,--the legends of the Mythic Christ, Buddha, Krishna,--mingling with the history of each, and crystallizing about each as an historical personage.

But these materialized stories pertain especially to the life of the Son of Man, a distinctive title, not of an individual but an office. When one attains this level and stands in this relation to humanity, then, as a representative of God, the story of the Logos in the Sun becomes his own indeed, for the facts underlying this story have been wholly realized in his spiritual life.

Here we learn the manner in which arose the story of the death, burial and resurrection of a crucified Savior. On the lines of the Solar-Myth and the Initiatory rites, the materializing tendency of man wrought out for itself, in each religion, an historical narrative of a personal Savior, who is virgin born, is crucified, rises from the dead, and finally ascends into heaven; or, the historicizing, may, in some instances, have been purposely done by those who knew,-

-the popular narrative being written for the multitude in such a way as to set forth the Mysteries allegorically. In either case,--and perhaps both methods played a part (we have abundant proof of the former and many indications of the latter),--the account symbolizes the inner doctrine and sets forth figuratively the occult teaching of the Gnosis. But the real meaning of the symbolical teaching of the Myth and Ritual has been practically lost sight of; most people to-day regard the narratives as the physical life history of individuals. However, there are some who are beginning to understand that the symbolical teaching of the death, burial, and resurrection are but typical of the soul's progress.

Jesus of Nazareth, like Buddha, Krishna, and many others, was draped with the stories of the Logos, and the salient events in the Sun-Myth become the salient events in his physical life. The symbols, once materialized, were attached to each Divine Teacher in turn, giving rise to the wonderful similarities in their respective biographies.

But let us not lose sight of the fact that the mystic birth, baptism, transfiguration, death, resurrection and ascension were realities in the life history of every Initiate. This drama is repeated in every soul that be-comes a Christ.

The story of the gospel was originally a religious romance intended for spiritual instruction, but the later bishops of the outer churches, not having the key to the inner meaning, accepted the romance as actual his-tory. It is said that "The 'common document' [which formed the basis of the canonical gospels] is to be traced to the sketch of an ideal life which was intended for purposes of propaganda, and which could be further explained to those who were ready for more definite instructions in the true nature of the

Christ-Mystery. To a certain extent it was based on some of the tradi-tions of the actual historic doings of Jesus, but the historical details were often transformed by the light of the mystery-teaching, and much was added in changed form concerning the drama of the Christ Mystery; al-legories and parables and actual mystery doings were woven into it, with what appears now to be a consummate art which has baffled for ages the intellect of the world, but which at the time was regarded by the writer as a modest effort at simplifying the spiritual truths of the Inner life, by putting them forward in the form of what we should now call a 'his-torical romance,' but which in his day was one of the natural methods of haggada and apocalyptic." (Did Jesus Live 100 Years B.C.? Mead, p. 422.)

The author of this romance never dreamed that the story would be taken otherwise than as he intended it--a symbol, but in the compilation of the canonical accounts much legend and historicized dogma was built around this original romance.

The mystic teaching in this way became accepted first as history and fi-nally as dogma. Irenaeus was one of the chief developers of the dogmas. The Gnostics contended that he and those like him who accepted the crude literal view, did not know the origin and meaning of these things. Papius and Marcion, who were earlier than Irenaeus, insisted that such scripture was not reliable as absolute history. The Gnostics knew how these scriptures were made and they possessed a "memory of the manner of things done and said from the earliest times, and looked with amazement on the narrow and cramping beliefs that the bishops of the outer churches were imposing on Christendom as the only truths of the Christ-revelation. . . This contention of the Gnostics, as of men earlier than Justin and Irenaeus, is still subjudice before the bar of history. It means a total reconstruction of the history of the origins." (G.R. 5. Mead in Theosoph1cal Review, March, '06.)

The Gnostics treated the gospel legends, not as history, but as symbolic of cosmic processes and the drama of Initiation. I have already shown that the Gnostics did not accept the crucifixion and resurrection of Jesus as historic facts. Justin Martyr also gives evidence that the early church did not understand these things in a literal sense. He says, "And when we say that the Word (Logos) which is the first begetting of God was begotten without intercourse,--Jesus Christ, our Master,--and that he was crucified, and was dead, and rose again and ascended into heaven, we bring forward no new thing beyond those among you who are called Sons of Zeus. For ye know how many sons the writers who are held in honor among you ascribe to Zeus:-- Hermes, the Word (Logos), who was the interpreter and teacher of all; and Asclepius, who was also a healer and was smitten by the bolt [of his sire] and ascended into heaven. . . [and many others ]." ( Quoted in Thrice Greatest Hermes, Mead, Vol. III, p. 217.) Justin Martyr here asserts that the Christians bring forward no new thing in the doctrines of Christ's death, resurrection, and ascension "beyond those among, you who are called the 'Sons of Zeus.'" The doctrine, then, was a part of the Mysteries, well known by all who had attained to the state of Sons of God. This mystery could not be understood by the uninitiated, and so Justin appeals to the Sons of Zeus, and assures them that he has no new doctrine. This is conclusive evidence that at the time of Justin Martyr, 140 to 160 A.D., these great spiritual realities in the Mystic life were not regarded by some, at least, as historical facts.

Justin further says, "But as to the Son of God called Jesus, even though he were only a man [born] in the common way, [yet] because of [his] wisdom is he worthy to be called Son of God; for all writers call God 'Father of men and gods.' And if we say [further] that he was also in a special way, beyond the common birth, begotten of God [as] Word (Logos) of God, let us have this in common with you who call Hermes the Word [Logos] who brings tidings from God." (Ibid, p. 217.)

The Sonship of Jesus, then, was considered the same as that of Hermes. And note also that "begotten of God" did not refer to physical birth, but to something beyond. Justin distinctly stated that Jesus was a man

born in the common way. This higher birth by which man was begotten of God, and so became a "Son," was not exceptional with Christianity. In fact, Justin Martyr wants it distinctly understood that he teaches nothing new, but merely claims for Jesus the distinctive title of a Son of God, in the same sense as were Hermes, Asclepius, Dionysus, and others, Sons of God, that is, he claimed Jesus was an Initiate.

Origen also is in accord with Justin Martyr. He speaks of the "mystery of the resurrection" and contrasts this inner doctrine, (which he says is not understood by unbelievers,) with the exoteric doctrine of the resurrection which was known to all and was an article of faith among many. (Origen Against Celsus, Book I, Ch. VII.) It is quite evident that there was a wide difference between the mystic doctrine of the crucifixion and resurrection, and the popular exoteric faith.

Thus studying the inner teaching of the Mysteries we see that Christ is not a unique personage, but the first fruits--the promise of man made perfect. The Initiate has ever been thus regarded, for to attain the Christ-state is salvation. "The stage of discipleship was to pass into that of Sonship. The life of the Son was to be lived among men till it was closed by the resurrection, and the glorified Christ became one of the perfected Saviors of the World." (Esoteric Christianity, Besant, p. 250.)

Every man is a potential Christ, and the purpose of evolution is to raise every human being to the sublime degree of a Master Christ.

## 9

## LECTURE VIII

THE ORIGIN AND HISTORY OF FREEMASONRY. The majority of the uninitiated believe that everything connected with Masonry is to be kept a secret. This is an error, for there are many books written on Masonry which are open to the perusal of all, whether they be members of or strangers to the Order. I shall divulge no pledged secrets.

The Eminent Masonic Scholars, Messrs. Stillson and Hughan, in introducing the "History of Freemasonry and Concordant Orders," plainly state that, "Neither is the work necessarily for Freemasons alone; for not a few of the chapters furnish excellent and suggestive reading for those who would like to know somewhat of the Brotherhood either prior to joining its ranks, or because of this eligible opportunity to peruse a reliable account of so venerable and pre-eminently respectable an Organization."

Except for some portions of the Ceremony--the signs and passwords-- which relate to the modes of recognition, there is nothing secret in Masonry.

There has been so much misunderstanding on this subject that perhaps it might be well to corroborate this statement. The same standard authority just cited says, "At the outset, therefore, it is well to point out that the Masonic fraternity is not, strictly speaking, a secret society, for it has neither secret aims nor constitutions. Everywhere its laws may be perused by 'friend and foe' alike, and its objects are exclusively those which are, and always have been, published to the world. It is private rather than secret; for, unless it be our esoteric customs, which relate, directly or indirectly, to our universal and special modes of recognition, we have no secrets."

Many absurd notions regarding Masonry have gained credence in the past, even among Masons themselves. We are pleased to see that modern Masonic writers are endeavoring to right these misconceptions. Formerly it was regarded as treason to speak to the profane the truth regarding the history of the Order. That certain exaggerated statements were made in the days when little was known of the history of the institution, gives no reason for a continuance of these errors.

There is no reason to-day for the pretensions that Freemasonry originated in the days of King Solomon, or with the Jewish Patriarchs, or that the fundamental doctrines of Masonry--the unity of God and the Immortality of the soul--were the exclusive possession of any one people or religion. Such claims were made before the science of comparative religions was so well known. For modern investigation of the world religions show us that these beliefs were world-wide, and held by all the great nations of antiquity before the Jewish nation was born, or Abraham had left the valley of the Euphrates

Neither is the old Masonic tradition tenable that all the knowledge of the ancient Mysteries and the present interior form of Freemasonry was derived from the Tyrian workmen at the building of King Solomon's Temple. There is no evidence that the Jews possessed this "interior form," or that Masonry itself included it before 1717 when it was introduced into the Order by those who had a knowledge of the Ancient Mysteries.

Masonry, then, is not a lineal descendant of the Mysteries; but is moulded upon them. The Reconstructionists built upon the ancient myths, using symbols known from the earliest days, and wove these symbols and myths derived from the Mysteries, into the symbolism of Solomon's Temple.

The traveling Freemasons of the Middle Ages may or may not have been descendants of the Dionysian artificers; of this we have no evidence, nor do we know the exact date of the beginning of the Masonic movement, but are assured it can lay claim to no great antiquity--the actual history of the Craft extending no further back than some six centuries. And then this early organization, prior to the reconstruction period of 1717, was something quite different from its present form--modern Masonry belng an entirely new departure.

The application of the term Freemasonry to the Ancient Mysteries, whether Jewish or Pagan, is then misleading; and the designation of the former as pure and the latter as spurious, is absurd and without any basis in fact. Both systems were derived from the same source and both are true; however, the Pagan antedated the Jewish by many thousands of years. It is curious what people will do and to what extremes they will go in support of a theological creed !

Although the origin of the Masonic movement is modern, we hold that it had its source in true Mysticism, and is one of the channels of the Mystic teaching. In corroboration of this let us note some of the connecting links between the esoteric schools of the early Christian centuries and the later Masonic movement.

The words of the well known Masonic authority, E. Macbean, are of interest in this connection. He says, "I may suggest that some portion at least of our symbolism may have come through a Templar source, Romanist, yet deeply tinged with Gnosticism; while at a later date the Lollards, (supposed to be inheritors of Manicheism), and who were but one of the many

religo-political societies with which Europe was honeycombed, possibly introduced or revived some of these teachings. . . One thing is certain, that satisfactory renderings of our symbols can only be obtained by a study of Eastern Mysticism; Kabbalistic, Hermetic, Pythagorean, and Gnostic. Down the centuries we find enrolled the names of philosophic teachers who veiled their doctrines in figures similar to those in vogue among the Rosicrucians and still more recent students, and often iden-

tical with the signs we blazon on the walls of our Lodges and Chapters."
(Hidden Sources of Masonry, Cooper-Oakley, pp. 34-35.)

One tradition traces Masonry to Manicheism or The Sons of the Widow. John Yarker, in speaking of this order, says, "About the year, 200, A. D., the most noteworthy Gnostic sect was a Persian branch of the Manichees; it was divided into three classes-- Auditors, Elect and Perfect, and the sect was ruled by twelve Apostles, with a thirteenth as President. . . The Rite had a Theosophical Gospel, which taught that the basis; of

all religion was one. In 657 they had changed their names to Paulicians, and later Cathari, Euchites, Bogomiles, and in still more recent times still, Lollards. . . They were a secret speculative society, with degrees, distinguished by signs, tokens and words like Freemasonry." (The Kneph, Vol. V, No. 4.)

This order was founded by Mani, as a restatement of the old truths of the Mysteries, and contained the true Gnosis. He combined the teachings of Zoroaster with those of Jesus--both being aspects of the same Wisdom,-

-but the mystery teaching had come to be regarded as heretical by the established Orthodoxy of both religions, consequently he was put to death by the Persians, and his disciples likewise slain by the Christians.

The Manicheans, from the fourth century, were bitterly persecuted by the Roman Church; the society, however, spread rapidly in spite of all opposition. Says Reghellina da Schio, a well known Italian Mason, "In the lifetime of Manes [Mani], his pupil, Herman, had spread his teaching in Eggpt, where the Coptic priests and other Christians mingled it with the Mysteries adopted from the Jews. . . It was through these same Coptic priests and the Eastern Christians that both the Mysteries of the Children of the Widow, and the cult of the Great Architect, came to us in consequence of apparently unforeseen events, and it will be seen that it was principally by means of the Crusades that they obtained a secure footing in the West. The Mysteries maintained their existence under the

name of the cult of the Great Architect of the Universe, a name that has its origin in the allegory of Hiram, which represented, in the Mysteries, 'the unknown God,' the Eternal. . .
The long time that elapsed during the war of the
Crusades gave them the opportunity of being admitted into all the Mysteries of the Children of the Widow. .
. The Crusaders who had been admitted to the mysteries of the Children of the Widow and mitiated therein, imparted them, on their return home, to their pupils in Europe." (Quoted in Hidden Sources of Masonry, p. 37.)

The secret teaching is supposed to have passed from the Templars to the Freemasons. Eclert traces the connection of the Manicheans with the Johannes Bruder of the West, and links them also to the German Building Corporations and Societies.

The Manicheans were known at different ages under different names. After the death of the founder there was a fusion of the Order with some of the leading Christian Gnostic sects, thus was further intermingled the two rich streams of Divine Wisdom: one coming from Egypt through Palestine, the other from India through Persia. The name of the external form, which preserved the secret science through the ages, was ever changing,

so we are not surprised to find one tradition tracing Freemasonry to the Gnostic Brotherhood of St. John, and it might equally as well be ascribed to the Albigenses, Johannite Christians, Troubadours, and a host of others, for all were possessors of tne same mystic tradition, and transmitted their knowledge from age to age. When persecuted under one name they veiled their mysteries under another.

The Cologne Record, which is dated 1535, bears witness that a secret society existed before 1440, under the name of the Brotherhood of St. John, and since then and up to 1535 under the title of St. John's Order of Freemasonry or Masonic Brotherhood. This Record contains the following passage: "The Brotherhood, or the Order of Freemason

Brothers, bound together according to St. John's holy rules; traces its origin neither from the Templars nor from any other spiritual or temporal Knightly Order, but it is older than all similar Orders, and has existed in Palestine and Greece, as well as in various parts of the Roman Empire. Before the Crusades our Brotherhood arose; at a time when in consequence of the strife between the sects teaching Christian morals, a small number of the Initiated - entrusted with the true teaching of virtue, and the sensible exposition of the secret teaching-- separated themselves from the mass." Of course, the authenticity of this Record is rejected by materialistic Masons, but is usually accepted as genuine by all Mystic Masons. Mr. Mackensie points out that the Record is referred to in the register of the Lodge at Hague, as there in existence, so, if it is a fraud, it is one of at least two centuries standing.

The mystic teaching of the Brotherhood of St. John must have been the same as that of the other mystic Orders, and the value of this Record is in the testimony it bears to the known existence of this secret teaching; whether Masonry received it from the Templars or from some older organization is not important.

Some contend that until the revival, in 1717, the mysteries of the craft were merely the peculiar methods or rules employed in their special art. This maybe partly true of the body as a whole, but that an inner occult teaching existed is quite evident. Gen. Pike says that "Among Freemasons of a certain class and limited in number, the same symbolism or a large part of the same, as afterwards placed in the degrees, did exist long before, perhaps some centuries before 1717." If they possessed the symbols they must have had a knowledge, in part at least, of their meaning. Again Gen. Pike says, "The art of building then stood above all other arts and made all others subservient to it.

It commanded the services of the most brilliant intellects and of the greatest artists. The old symbolism was embodied in the churches and cathedrals, and some of these were adorned with figures and devices

which would never have been tolerated there if the priesthood had known what they meant to the Adepts." This proves their possession of occult knowledge.

Mr. Findel sums up the opinions of the leading Freemasons of Germany as follows: "The Grand Lodge of Germany further assumes, that in the Building Fraternities of the Middle Ages, besides their art, a secret science was carried on, the substratum of which was a real Christian Mystery, serving as a preparatory or elementary school and stepping stone to that and the St. John's Masonry, which latter was not a mere system of moral philosophy, but closely allied and connected with this mystery. It was conceded, that the Freemasonry of our days, (St. John's Freemasonry), sprang from the Building Fraternities of the Middle Ages, but at the same time asserted that in the early ages there existed a secret society which strove to compass the perfecting of the human race, precisely in the same manner, and employing similar means, as did the Swedish system, which in fact only followed in the wake of its predecessor, being concealed in the Building Fraternities, so that our society did not arise from them, but made itself a way through them.

The secret science, the mystery, was very ancient

indeed. This mystery formed the secret of the Higher Degrees of the Rite, which were not merely kept hidden from the rest of the confederation, but also from the members of the inferior degrees of the system itself. This mystery was fully confirmed by documents, which the Grand Lodge of Germany had in its keeping.   This

secret legend is the same as that of the Carpocratians, which is that Jesus chose some of the Apostles and confided to them a secret science, which was transmitted afterwards to the priests of the Order of the Knights Templars, and through them to the Building Fraternities, down to the present Freemasons of the Swedish Rite. . .The Swedish system teaches that there have been men of all nations who have worshipped God in spirit and in truth, and surrounded by idolatry and superstition, have yet preserved their purer faith.

Separate from the world, and unknown to it, this Wisdom has been preserved by them and handed down as a mystery. In the time of the Jews they made use of the Essenes, in which sect Jesus was brought up, and spent the greater part of his life.

"Having been instructed by Him in a more perfect knowledge of Holy Things, they had, amid persecution, taught in silence that which was committed to their keeping. At the period of the Saracens and the Crusades they were so greatly oppressed that they must ultimately have sought for protection from without. As fate, however, would have it, seven of them, Syriac Christians, pursued by unbelievers, near Bastrum, were rescued by the Knights-Templars, and afterwards taken under their protecton. When they had lived there for a

certain time they begged for permission to dwell with the Canons or Prebendaries of Jerusalem, as the life there led agreed better with their own inclinations and habits. This was accorded them, and Andreas Montebarrensis effected a union of these Syrians with the Canons, to whom, out of gratitude, they imparted; all their science, and so completely did they make the priests of the order the depositories of their secrets that they kept and handed them over to others under certain conditions. Thus, this secret knowledge lived on in the very heart of the Order of Knights Templars till its, abolition. The clergy were dispersed with the persecution that ensued, but as the secular arm did not touch them, as it did the Knights, they managed to rescue many of their secret writings, and when the Knights sought refuge in Scotland, they founded a Chapter at Aberdeen, the first Prior of which was Petrus de Bononia. The science was disseminated from this place, but very cautiously, first to Italy, then to the extreme north (Sweden and Russia ?), and France." (History of Freemasonry, Findel, pp. 299-310.)

To be sure, Mr. Findel quotes this history in a rather skeptical way, but the claim of a secret teaching is too well attested to be seriously questioned. The Middle Ages were honey-combed with mystic societies, each an instrument used in keeping alive and handing along the mystic teaching under various disguises. If Masonry had no part in this work, it was truly an exception to the many societies that existed from the 4th.

to the 18th. centuries.

The early history of Freemasonry is very meagre, owing perhaps to the nature of the organization. The earliest records of actual lodge meetings were in 1599, but there are copies of "Old Charges" and laws dating from the 14th. century.

It does not appear from the oldest manuscript that they used signs, tokens, and words, such as later on were employed to secure recognition; however, such may have been the case. There were certain secrets which pertained to the art of building, which the members of the Lodge were bound to keep, and it was these trade secrets which gave to the Order its monopoly. But in the course of time the strict regulation of the guilds relaxed and there gradually grew up another body of operatives, which succeeded in breaking down the monopoly, thus opening the way for the purely Speculative Society.

The term Freemason, which originally meant a worker in free stone, came later on to be applied to all "Craftsmen who had obtained their freedom as Masons to work in Lodges with the Fraternity after due apprenticeship and passing as Fellow Crafts." As early even as the oldest "Charges" persons not operative

Masons were admitted to the Order and were designated by the term "Accepted," to distinguish them from the working Masons, for many of this class were attracted to Masonry by the moral principles, and perhaps the mystic knowledge of the Fraternity. Some of these were men of learning, and it was this class undoubtedly that had much to do with the reconstruction of the Order.

The introduction of this "Speculative" membership; that is, those who did not follow the trade as a means of livelihood, proved a most fortunate thing for the preservation of the Order at a time when the old "Charges" had practically ceased to be influential. Had this not been done it is doubtful if the Institution of Freemasonry would have been in existence to-day.

Speculative Masonry existed as far back as the oldest "Charges," but the proportion which the Speculative element bore to the Operative is not known. From the few records we have of the 17th. century, it would seem that at that time the great majority were Speculative Freemasons, although some bodies were chiefly Operative.

We learn from the old records that Apprentices served seven years, and that being passed to Fellow Crafts depended upon the result of an examination as to their operative skill, and likewise the passing of Fellow Crafts to Master Masons. Of course, this did not apply to the honorary members. Apprentices were members and exercised all the privileges as such, just the same as Fellow Crafts and Masters, for at that time the separate Masonic degrees had not come into existence. Three grades or classes were recognized, but this did not signify esoteric stages, and we find no intimations of two or more degrees being worked before the "revival" of 1717.

By the latter part of the 17th century Masonry in England had begun to retrograde. The Society became so commercial that it applied merely to selfish gain, causing some who were more deeply interested in the Order to realize that something must be done to prevent total extinction of the Fraternity. The two moving spirits were Dr. Anderson and Dr. Desaguliers and at their hands the Order saw a complete change in 1717. During that year four Lodges met in London on June 24, and formed the premier Grand Lodge of the World. This, however, did not include the Masonic body at York. The York Masons remained independent, and formed in 1725 a Grand Lodge of their own, called the Grand Lodge of all England. This body continued until 1790, but it never chartered Lodges outside of England.

Dr. Anderson and Dr. Desaguliers, together with other old members chosen for their ability, were designated by the Order to formulate a new and better method of the history, charges, regulations, etc. As the result

of their work we have the Free and Accepted Masonry, founded on the apochryphal legend of "Hiram," and the "Symbolism of Solomon's Temple."

In the formation of degrees many of the customs of the ancient Mysteries were adopted. The third or Master's Degree, based upon the "Hiram" legend, came into use about 1723, in fact, the whole degree system was the work of the Reconstructionists.

Says Dr. Mackey, "It is now the opinion of the best scholars, that the division of the Masonic system into degrees was the work of the Revivalists of the beginning of the 18th century; that before that period there was but one degree, or rather one common platform of ritualism; and that was the division into Masters, Fellows, and Apprentices was simply a division of ranks, there being but one Initiation for all." (Art Degrees, Mackey's Encyclopedia.)

W.H. Hughan says, "I have carefully perused all the known Masonic manuscript, from the fourteenth century down to A.D. 1717 (of which I have either seen the originals or have certified copies), and have not been able to find any reference to three degrees." (Quoted in "Four Old Lodges," p. 40.)

Mr. Gould, another well known Masonic writer, says that there is no evidence to indicate the existence of the "Second degree, as now practiced until after the year 1717, nor of the Third degree until the year 1735." (Quoted by C.F. Francis in M.P.G.M. Address, Philadelphia, 1888, from Gould's Concise History. )

W.J.B. MacLeod Moore, Supreme Grand Master "ad Vitum" of the Sovereign Great Priory of Canada, also says, "Historical investigation clearly demonstrates that in 1717 the present system of degrees was entirely unknown. Originally there was but one degree of Initiation, containing all the elements of the degrees now practiced--the names of 'Entered Apprentice,' 'Fellow Craft' and 'Master Mason,' being merely the designation of the classes of workmen, not of degrees or steps--the actual Society or Fraternity being composed of 'Fellows;' for in the oldest records, constitutions and charges, there is not the slightest allusion to these separate degrees, nor any to the legend of 'Hiram Abif.' The four old Lodges remaining in London in 1717 were composed entirely of 'Fellows.'" (History of Freemasonry and Concordant Orders, p. 753.)

The symbolism and legends adopted by the Revisionists and worked into the degrees, are chiefly those of the Ancient Mysteries. The immediate source fram which this material was derived is not definitely known. Many have thought that the Reconstructionists derived it from the Rosicrucians and Bacon's "New Atlantis." Mr. Hughan

says that Wigston's books on "Bacon, Shakespeare and the Rosicrucians" and "Francis Bacon, Poet, Prophet and Philosopher," contain Rosicrucian and Baconic ideas, which influenced the Masonic Reconstructionists of 1717. He again says that "The New Atlantis seems to be, and probably is, the key to the modern ritual of Freemasonry." (Ibid, p. XXXI.)

Masonry is thoroughly Hermetic and Kabbalistic, and the framers of these degrees were evidently Kabbalistic and Hermetic philosophers, and well acquainted with all these works and other mystic writngs.

Mr. Singleton, 33d degree, Sec. M. W. Grand Lodge, District of Columbia, says, "The Kabbalists were the inventors of the rituals of the original degrees, and Kabbalistic scholars in France and Germany have multiplied the degrees by elaborating upon the 'legends' of the first three. . .There was originally in Speculative Masonry but one ritual, which was very simple; out of that one trunk have grown all the branches, and the fruit from these bears the resemblance of Hermeticism and the Kabbalah. . . The Third degree, the Royal Arch, and the Select of 27, are all designed to imitate the ancient Mysteries." (Ibid, p. 105).

Mr. Moore, already quoted, says, "Some of these rites would appear to be derived from the Hermetic philosophy of the German school, of which no proof exists; but when philosophers, with others, joined the Craft Lodges in the 17th century, they may have introduced some of their Hermetic Rosicrucian symbols into Masonry." (Ibid, p. 759) .

Gen. Pike, the eminent American Masonic authority, says that to "The men of intelligence who belonged to one of the lodges in 1717, is to be ascribed the authorship of the third degree and the introduction of

Hermetic and other symbols into Masonry; they formed the three degrees for the purpose of communicating their doctrines, veiled by their symbols except to those fitted to receive them, and to give to all others trite moral explanations of them which they could receive." The plan was worked out by these Reconstructionists and formally approved and accepted in 1723, becoming known as the new constitution, and is the Freemasonry of

to-day. (Anderson's Constitutions, 1723).

In 1730 a work called "Masonry Dissected," appeared. This purported to be a revelation of Free and Accepted Masonry. As the result of this many spurious Lodges were formed. The Grand Lodge endeavored to thwart this by introducing certain changes in the pass-words, etc. These alterations caused much dissatisfaction, and many withdrew from the regular Lodges and formed Lodges of their own. These seceders finally formed an independent

body in 1751, and assumed the name "Ancient York Masons." They claimed to have preserved the old forms-- thus the name "Ancient," and they called the regular Grand Lodge the "Moderns." Both Grand Lodges were prosperous and extended their influence even into America, thus producing dissension not only at home but abroad. The strife between these two Grand Lodges continued until 1813, when a union was effected under the title of the United Grand Lodge. A union was also effected in America, thus ending the schism, and to constitute a regular mode of work a union degree was adopted. The Grand Lodge of Ireland was formed in 1728, and the Grand Lodge of Scotland in 1736.

There is no uniformity in the degree system in the different countries. To the three symbolic degrees, others have been added from time to time, but there has been no uniformity in their acceptance. The Royal Arch appeared about 1740, but by whom it was founded is not known, though it is clearly of English origin. There is no record of its being worked in Chapters until 1762, when a chapter of the Royal Arch was formed at York. It became the fourth degree in the Ancient Grand

Lodge system. The "Moderns" did not recognize this degree or adopt it officially until 1767. Upon the union it became a part of the English Rite.

The Mark degree also originated about this time. It was formerly conferred in England under Royal Arch warrants, but later was governed by an independent Grand Lodge of its own.

The Past Master degree is undoubtedly one of evolution. It was originally worked in Craft Masonry, being conferred on the newly elected Master when about to be installed. This degree was finally adopted as a separate degree by the Royal Arch system, and transferred from the Lodge to the Chapter. Although its origin is obscure, it was conferred during the latter part of the 18th century. The Most Excellent degree is also obscure in origin, but we find it also conferred in the latter part of the 18th century. In many instances the higher degrees were worked under Lodge warrants by those interested, without interference from the Grand Lodge. The brethren concerned came together and conferred the higher degrees. They were at first purely side degrees, but after a time they became organized independently. Royal Arch Masonry separated from Blue Lodge Masonry, organized itself and adopted or invented the four degrees just considered, and began an independent existence. In the same way the Royal and Select Masters separated themselves from the Lodge of Perfection and formed Councils, and finally organized Grand Councils and became also independent.

As already stated, there is no uniformity in the different countries concerning these higher degrees.

The system in England is unknown in France and Germany. The American system, known as the York Rite, consists of the Craft degrees or Blue Lodge, the Royal Arch Chapter, the Council and the Knights Templars, and is peculiar to this country. It was formulated by Thomas Smith Webb, who, with his associates constructed, out of the-conglomeration of the work of the "Ancients" and "Moderns" that had previously been established in this country, a new work, which Cross and others afterwards embellished. Webb tried to show that he had adopted the true work of the Ancient York Masons, but it is well known that the claim is without foundation.

In concluding this chapter we will give in order the various degrees that constitute the standard Masonic work in this country.

They are the Symbolic degrees of the Blue Lodge-- Entered Apprentice, Fellow Craft and Master Mason.

The Capitular degrees of the Royal Arch Chapter-- Mark Master, Past Master, Most Excellent Master and the Royal Arch.

The Cryptic degrees of the Council--Royal Master, Select Master and Super-Excellent Master.

The Chivalric degrees of the Commandry of Knights Templars--Knight of the Red Cross, Knight Templar and Knight of Malta, and

The Philosophic degrees of the Scottish Rite system, divided into--a Lodge of Perfection, a Council Princes of Jerusalem, a Chapter of Rose Croix, a Council of Kadosh, a Consistory and the Supreme Council.

The history of the Knights Templars will be considered in our next lecture, together with that of the Ancient and Accepted Scottish Rite.

## 10

## LECTURE IX

THE ORIGIN AND HISTORY OF THE KNIGHTS TEMPLARS AND THE ANCIENT AND ACCEPTED SCOTTISH RITE.

We will first consider the Military Order of the Knights Templars of the Crusades. This organization was originally called the Order of the Temple, and was founded in 1118-1119 A.D., by nine Benedictine Monks, who resided in Monasteries at Jerusalem. The object of the Order was the defense of the Holy Sepulcher and the protection of the Christian pilgrims who visited the sacred shrine. The holy place had been desecrated and the Christians persecuted by both Saracen and Turk. The Christian Monks joined the Patriarch of Jerusalem in guarding the approach to the city, and lived under the Benedictine rule, fighting for the cause of the Church.

The Patriarch assigned them quarters in the palace of the Latin Kings of Jerusalem, sometimes called Solomon's Temple, and it was this that gave the Templar name to the Order.

The new Order rendered valiant service to the pilgrims and others in need; their fame spread rapidly and their ranks as rapidly increased by recruits from the religious fraternities in Europe, members of the French nobility, and then from all classes of society. These recruits were organized by skillful military leaders and before long became renowned in the art of war. The Order was strictly a religious body and was composed of three classes,--Knights, Chaplains and Serving Brothers. A council was held in 1128 to determine the statutes of the Order. Rules of discipline and obligations numbering seventy-two were adopted. At a later date they were elaborated into a more complete ritual.

In our last lecture we mentioned that the early Templars possessed a secret doctrine. The early Freemasons also taught in secret, making it difficult to trace one without mentioning the other. I need here only to recall that the secret science had passed along from age to age, until received by the Knights Templars. According to the record of the German Lodges the Templars received their mystic teaching from certain Syriac Christians, but of what particular doctrine, cult or order they do not state. Perhaps they were members of the Brotherhood of St. John, which, according to the Cologne Record, possessed a mystic teaching or perhaps they were members of the Johannian Christians; again, perhaps these two Societies may have been of the same or a very similar order. The Johannites were also called "Christians of the East." There is a tradition that traces the secret teaching of the Templars to the Johannites, so it is more than probable that the Syriac Christians were members of this Brotherhood.

This tradition, as given by Gen. Pike, states that "There existed at that period in the East a sect of Johannite Christians, who claimed to be the only true Initiates into the real Mysteries of the religion of the Savior. They pretended to know the real history of Jesus the Anointed, and, adopting in part the Jewish traditions and the tales of the Talmud, they held that the facts recounted in the Evangels are but allegories.

. . The Johannites ascribe to St. John the foundation of their Secret Church, and the Grand Pontiff's of the Sect assumed the title of Christos, Anointed or Consecrated, and claimed to have succeeded one another from St. John by an uninterrupted succession of pontifical powers. He who, at the period of the foundation of the Order of the Temple, claimed these imaginary prerogatives, was named Theoclet." (Morals

and Dogma, Pike, p. 816.) Theoclet was acquainted with Hugh de

Payens, the founder of the Order of the Temple, and initiated him into the Johannian Mysteries and appointed him his successor.

Now if the Brotherhood of St. John and the Johannian Christians are the same, then both the Templars and the Freemasons received their secret doctrine from the same order. It is claimed by some, however, that the mystic teaching passed to the Masons from the Templars. This may or may not have been the case, but that they were closely allied is evident from the fact that upon the destruction of the old Templar Order many of its members took refuge with the Freemasons.

The secret statutes of the Templars were preserved, not only by oral tradition, but were also written, in part at least. Dr. Prutz says, "Gervais de Beauvias saw at one of the heads of the Orders a little book with the Statutes of the Order of 1128, which was shown without thinking, and he knew that the same man had also possessed another book about which he was very mysterious and which he 'would not show any one for all the world.'" ( Geheimelehre des Templherren Ordens, p. 45.) W.J. MacLeod Moore, 33rd degree, in speaking of the Temple Order, says, "Their Rulers arrogated to themselves a higher degree of knowledge in all things, and taught in their secret conclaves, where none but the most trusted members were admitted, that the Papal power was a false and dangerous assumption of authority over the minds and consciences of men, and that very many of the dogmas of Rome were gross and childish superstitions. They also cultivated and asserted more liberal views of faith and religion than were current at the time, being well versed in the Mysteries, legends, learning and traditions of the peoples they had come in contact with in the East." (History of Freemasonry and Concordant Orders, p. 765.)

The evidence that the early Templar Order possessed a secret doctrine being conclusive, we will now return to the historical development.

The Order spread rapidly and was soon established in every kingdom of Latin Christendom. The part which the Templars took in the Crusades is too well known to need reiteration, for from that time on the history of the Templars was the history of the Crusades.

When the Crusades terminated the Templars returned to their numerous Preceptories in Europe, as the Order was of no further use as a military body. Their great wealth and power aroused the jealously of Philip IV. of France, who coveted the possessions of the Order, and the Pope distrusted its fidelity to the Papacy. A bitter hatred was engendered by many acts of insubordination against the king's arbitrary authority,

and he set about to work their destruction; to this end calumnies of every description were circulated, they were charged with heresy and all manner of crimes.

Philip enlisted the support of Pope Clement V., who owed his papal tiara to the King's gold or influence, and the overthrow was brought about. The work of suppression was too heartless to recite. Many were cast into prison, and tortured to confess crimes of which they were ignorant, and finally were burned to death upon fagots. The Grand Master De Molai was seized while in Paris by special invitation of Pope Clement, cast into prison, where he was kept seven years, and at last taken out and burned at the stake. On May 2, 1312, Clement issued his famous Bull transferring the estates of the Templars, except those in Spain and Portugal, to the Knights of St. John.

Thus perished the Order of the Temple. What became of the thousands of Templars upon the suppression of the Order is not definitely known. Some may have joined the Order of St. John of Jerusalem, upon which the confiscated lands of the Templars had been conferred, and some, as already intimated, may have taken refuge in the Guilds of Stone Masons.

Many reject this latter theory as being without "historic foundation," but W.S. Perry, 32nd degree, says regarding this, "We do not question this statement as it stands. History fails to record much that actually occurs, much that subsequent ages would gladly know. We see no reason, however, for the assertion, so often made of late years, that any connection between a Chivalric Order, such as the Knights Templars, and a fraternity of Operative Masons, such as certainly existed in Mediaeval times, is out of the range of possibility." (Ibid, p. 140.) Mr. Perry then goes on to argue that the Guilds were known and even employed by the Knights Templars in the construction of their Churches, Preceptories, and strongholds, all over Europe and the Holy Land, and when they were despoiled they would naturally seek protection among the body with which they had already a certain connection.

Henry E. Manning, Cardinal Archbishop of Westminster, says, "As far back as the 12th century, the Lodges of the Guild enjoyed the special protection of the Knights Templars. It is easy in this way to understand how the symbolical allusion to Solomon and His Temple might have passed from the Knights into the Masonic formulary. In this way, too, might be explained how, after the suppression of the Order of the Temple, some of the recalcitrant Knights, maintaining their influence over the Freemasons, would be able to pervert what hitherto had been a harmless ceremony into an elaborate ritual that shoukl impart some of the errors of the Templars to the Initiated." (Ibid, p. 144.)


This Catholic writer may know whereof he speaks, as it is generally supposed that Catholic scholars have access to certain records not accessible to others, therefore, it is not improbable that the old Order continued to exist within the Guilds of Stone Masons. It is also said that when the time came that they could safely proclaim the continuance of their Order, they instituted the Rite of Strict Observance and proved their gratitude for the protection afforded by receiving members only from the ranks of Freemasonry.

But it is also not unlikely, as pointed out by Mr. Moore, that "Small organizations were kept up in many places, and the hope cherished that it would be possible to revive the Order. A great and extensive organization could not wholly have lost its vitality and died out without a struggle." (Ibid, p. 768.) It is related of the Chief of the doomed Order that before his execution he instituted what afterward came to be called Occult, Hermetic, or Scottish Masonry; that the Order, while seeming to die, nevertheless lived under other names, and was revealed to those who proved themselves worthy to be trusted. According to these traditions the real lineal descendants of the Old Chivalric Orders are the Scottish Rite and the Strict Observance.

Let us consider for a moment this Rite of the Strict Observance.

It is common with a certain class of Masonic writers to pronounce the leading spirits of the Strict Observance, dupes and charlatans. But the long list of scholars, nobles, and officers of high standing who have belonged to this Order must preclude any such classification.

The reason for such stigmatization is that the members were students of Mysticism, and believed that there is hidden in Masonry an occult and mystic tradition which is the true history of spiritual evolution. Many of these members of the Strict Observance also belonged to the Rosicrucians and other allied bodies, and all were seeking the old "Strait Gate" and "Narrow Path" that leads to Wisdom.

One of the most striking personages of this period is Charles Gotthelf, a nobleman born in 1722. "He entered the Masonic Order in 1742, when at Frankfort-on-Main. In the next year he is said to have established a Lodge at Paris, and while staying with the French Army he became acquainted with the heads of a Rite which pretended to be, in its higher degrees, the continuation of the famous Order of Knights Templars.

According to his repeated declarations, maintained even on his death bed, he was received into this Order, in Paris, by Lord Kilmarnock, Grand Master of Scotland, a Jacobite nobleman, on which occasion Lord Clifford acted as Prior. He was presented to a very high member

of the Order, a mysterious personage called only 'the Knight of the Red Feather.' Perhaps this was Prince Charles Edward himself. Von Hund supposed him to be the Supreme Grand Master of the Order, and was appointed by him coadjutor of the Seventh Province of the Order (Germania Inferior). Hund visited Scotland also, where he was bidden to raise the Order in Germany, together with the then Master of the Seventh Province, de Marschall, whom he always considered his predecessor.

Marschall had founded Lodges at Altenburg and Naumburg, but found only in the latter men worthy of being led further, viz., to be received into the Templar degrees." (This is a summary by Cooper-Oakley in "Traces of a Hidden Tradition" of an article in the "Transctions of Logge Quator Coronati" No. 2076.)

Reghellini says of Von Hund: "In 1756 the wars had caused the Prussian (Masonic) Lodges to be abandoned. Baron de Hund, who had received the High Templar's Degree in the Chapter of Clermont at Paris, on returning to Berlin declared that he had been raised to the dignity of Grand-Master of the Templars by M.Marschall, who called himself the successor of the G.'.G.'. Master Templars by uninterrupted transmission from the time of Jacques de Molai; that Marschall on his death-bed had delegated this high dignity to him, and had declared him his successor; transmitting to him all his powers and dignities. He did not omit to give Hund a list of all the names of the Templar Grand Masters, which must therefore have been a curious contrast to the list of the Order of the Temple of Paris. Hund placed himself at the head of the German reformers; he persuaded them that his Rite would restore Freemasonry to its ancient brilliancy and its former splendor. . . His principles were altogether philosophical. . . He maintains that these Pontiff's are the only Priests of the True Light, the Worshipers of God, and the disciples of the pure doctrines of Jesus and of John." ("Traces of a Hidden Tradition," 82.)

In this connection we need to note one Johann Augustus Starck, a teacher of Oriental languages and a student of theology and philosophy. He had held many public positions, among others that of interpreter of Oriental manuscript at the Royal Library in Paris. Mrs. Cooper-Oakley says, "Starck held that the mystic traditions of the Knights Templars, derived by them from those still older fraternities

with whom they had come in contact in the East, were preserved among the clericals of that Order who had cherished their unbroken continuity until his days, and he announced that he was in communication with certain Superiors, or Chiefs of the Order." (Ibid p. 84.)
R. F. Gould, a well known English authority, writing on the Strict Observance, says, "On February 17th, 1767,

some Masons, chief amongst whom may be mentioned Von Vegesack, Von Bohnen and Stark, founded at Wismar the Lodge of the 'Three Lions,' and attached thereto a Scots Lodge, 'Gustavus of the Golden Hammer.' Shortly

afterward they added a hitherto unknown body, a Clerical Chapter. To these brethren we are indebted for the historical fiction [sic] that the Knights Templars were divided into military and sacerdotal members; that the latter possessed all the secrets and mystic learning of the Order; and that they had preserved a continuous existence down to the eighteenth century. Stark claimed to be the emissary of these Clerical Templars, asserted their and his own superiority over the Secular Knights, and offered, on his claims being acknowledged, to impart their valuable secrets to Von Hund and his disciples. Stark (1741-1816) was a student of Gottingen, and a very learned man, an Oriental linguist of great attainments, and had held scientific appointments in St. Petersburg, Paris, Wismar and elsewhere." (History of Freemasonry, Gould, V., p. 104)

Gould regards Stark as an impostor, but like many other materialistic critics who reject the tradition, he offers no proof of its falsity.
In reply to the criticism that the Knights Templars could not have continued to exist for 438 years unknown to the outside world, Stark says, "If he [Dr. Biester] had been somewhat better acquainted with ecclesiastical history, he would have found not only one, but several religious bodies, which under far more violent opposition and persecution than those endured by the Knights Templars, have secretly continued to exist for a longer period than four hundred and fifty years." (Traces of a Hidden Tradition in Masonry, p. 86.)

This view is upheld by C. W. King, a modern writer of note, who, speaking of the Templars, says, "Considering how widely the Order has spread. . . it would be a mere absurdity to believe that all its traditions, were swept away at one stroke by the suppression of the Templars in the year 1307." (The Gnostics and Their Remains, King, p. 399.)

Stark shows the large number of scholars m his day who accepted the tradition. Can it be that all these were dupes and charlatans?

We must now pass to a brief consideration of the Order itself. Ragon, a noted Masonic writer, in speaking of the Strict Observance, says that in Germany a body was formed, "Approaching more nearly to the true institution than the ordinary Freemasons. The study of the Kabbalah, of the Philosophers' Stone and of Necromancy or the invocation of spirits, occupied them chiefly, because according to them all these sciences formed the system and the object and end of the ancient mysteries of which Freemasonry is the sequel."- ( Quoted from Orthodoxie Maconnique, Ragon, p. 210, by Mr. Cooper-Oakley in Hidden Tradition, p. 88.)

It was the-higher grades of the Strict Observance that took up the study of Alchemy, etc., there being, according to our author just quoted, seven grades into which the system was divided.


Much more might be said, but this is sufficient to show that in the early days of the Modern Knights Templars there were many who recognized the existence of the secret doctrine.

As to the origin of the Knights Templars of to-day, and their connection with Freemasonry, various theories have been proposed. Some contend that the movement was the result of the numerous works of the 17th and 18th centuries on occult philosophy, and that upon the dispersion of the Order of St. John and the Templars of Scotland, the secret ceremonies and principles were obtained and promulgated, which directly led to the revival of the Chivalric Orders under the impression that they were of Masonic origin.

Others hold that the present Order originated from the High Grades of

Freemasonry, the Hermetic, or Scottish system, and was grafted on to Freemasonry by Baron Hund in 1754. Few, if any, would maintain today that the present organization of Knights Templars is a lineal descendant of the old Chivalric Order. The Knights Templars of the present, in common with Masons in general, make no claim to mystic knowledge, and but few in the Order even know that such a Wisdom-science ever existed.

The degrees of the American system of the Knights Templars are the Knight of the Red Cross, Knight Templar, and Knight of Malta. The Red Cross is not embraced in the English, Continental or Canadian systems. The Templar degrees have been used in connection with Freemasonry for about a century. Says W.J.B. MacLeod Moore, "Although the Templar degrees have been in connection with Freemasonry for about a century past, it does not follow that they previously had any such connection. It was only about that time, or a few years earlier, that the error was made in Great Britain and Ireland of adding the chivalric Templar Order to the Masonic systems." (History of Freemasonry and Concordant Orders, p. 744.) The Templar degrees, like the other side degrees, were first conferred under Blue Lodge Warrants, which simply means that Masons possessing those degrees came together in their Lodges and worked them. In the course of time Chapters and Encampments were organized, and Templarism took on a more independent and permanent form.

We believe with Mr. Moore that it was an error to merge the Templar degrees into the Masonic system. In England the Templar system has always been kept separate from the Craft degrees. The Royal Arch is there considered the climax of Freemasonry. There is also a difference due to the fact that the English degrees are based upon the old Templar ceremonies, while the American system is based upon. the craft degrees. This, makes the American system broader and more in harmony with the spirit of Freemasonry, although it is still partly sectarian. This sectarianism is not in accord with the ancient landmarks and genius of Masonry. If we have the right to Christianize Masonry, so have Moslems,

Buddhists, and all other religious sects, a right to transform it to fit their creeds; such transformations and limitations deprive Masonry of its true spirit and universal character, and should such a process become general Masonry itself would soon be destroyed.

The Templar system should have stood alone on its own merits and principles. It should have been left as a series of side degrees

for Masons professing Christian principles. The very name "Masonic Templarism" is a misnomer--the sectarian character of the one is not in accord with the universal character of the other. This declaration does not cast any reflection upon the Templar degrees; in fact, we consider them among the best and most inspiring of the American system; however, we believe they should have remained separated from a non-sectarian body. "It is a mistake," to again quote Mr. Moore, "to connect Templarism with Freemasonry."

Frederic Speed, 33rd degree Past R. E. Grand Commander, Miss., is of the same opinion. He says, "If, then, anywhere the door of any degree is closed against him who believes in one God and the soul's immortality, on account of other tenets of his faith, that degree is not Freemasonry. That the Templar degrees [properly] form no part of Masonry, we have the declaration of the reputed author of the American Rituals, Thomas Smith Webb, who, in 1812, and several subsequent editions of his 'Freemason's Monitor,' says, 'Although the several orders of Knighthood are conferred both in Europe and America, reputedly under the sanction of Masonic assemblies,' they 'compose no part of the system of Freemasonry.' " He tells us that in America they are conferred as "honourary degrees." Mr. Speed continues, "It is time for intelligent Masons to divest themselves of the superlatively ridiculous and often exploded idea that there is any connection between what we now know as Templarism and the Fraternity of Free and Accepted Masons, except that which is found in the restriction of its membership to those who have first received the several degrees of Masonry. . . It is entirely compatible with all the obligations of Masonry that a Mason should be a Templar, and we do not derogate from our standing as Masons, when we take upon ourselves the additional vows of the Knights Templars; but this does not make Templarism Masonry, nor do we add anything to the dignity and high character of the Order by making the assertion that it is." (Ibid, p. 735)

ANCIENT AND ACCEPTED SCOTTISH RITE.

The Ancient and Accepted Scottish Rite or Scottish Masonry did not originate in Scotland, as its name might lead one to suppose. It was derived from a body in France, formerly known as "The Emperors of the East and West," who organized in 1758, in Paris, a Rite called "The Rite of Perfection," consisting of twenty-five degrees, to which eight or more were subsequently added.

The immediate source from which the French Masons derived these Rites is unknown, but it is held by some that they are the lineal descendants of the ancient Order of the Temple. Before the death of Grand Master Jacques de Molai, and while he was in prison awaiting execution, he instituted several Metropolitan Lodges, one of which was at Paris, and it was from this source that Scottish Masonry was derived. Gen. Pike, the great authority on the Scottish Rite, accepts this view. The name itself is supposed to have come from a number of Scottish Masons who were in France at the time of the organization.

A Grand Lodge was formed at Charleston, South Carolina, in 1783, a Supreme Council, 33rd degree, in 1801; and the Rite has been called by its present name, Ancient and Accepted Scottish Rite, since that

date.

The Rite is founded on the Symbolic degrees, and is conferred only on Master Masons. Its degrees begin with the 4th and extend to the 33rd. They are conferred in subordinate bodies as follows: The Lodge of Perfection--4th to 14th inclusive; the Council of Princes of Jerusalem--15th and 16th; the Chapter of Rose Croix--17th and 18th; the Consistory of Sublime Princes of the Royal Secret--19th to 32nd except in the Southern Jurisdiction where the 19th. to 30th. degrees constitute a Council of Kadosh and their Consistory begins with the 31st. degree; and the Supreme Council, whose officers are Active 33rd. degree Masons. There is also an Honourary 33rd. degree conferred by the Supreme Council as a merit for distinguished service in the-Fraternity.

The moral teaching of these degrees is exemplary and the dramatic effect of the work is beyond comparison. We have neither time nor space to consider the system in detail, but there are certain teachings connected with some of the degrees to which your special attention is directed. We refer to those which, by some, are thought to be sectarian in character, and therefore opposed to the original plan of the Reconstructionists-- to lay a broad foundation for the ceremonies which would admit men of all religions. It is to be regretted that such a cosmopolitan basis could not have been maintained.

We need to remember, however, that Masonry is symbolic and the legends, even of the so-called sectarian degrees, are symbols used to set forth an inner truth, and are not in themselves necessarily sectarian, even when appropriated by a special religion, for they are essentially universal, and belong to general religion.

To illustrate more fully, Dr. Mackey, in speaking of the Cryptic degrees, which are based upon the legend of the Sacred Vault, says, "To support this legend there is no historic evidence and no authority except that of the Talmudic writers. It is clearly a mythical symbol, and as such we must accept it. . . . Like every other myth and allegory of Masonry, the historical relation may be true, or it may be false; it may be founded on fact, or be the invention of imagination; the lesson is still there, and the symbolism teaches it, exclusive of the history." (Encyclopedia of Freemasonry, p. 852.)

Gen. Pike also emphasizes this principle. In speaking of the legend upon which the degree of the Royal Arch is based, he says, "It is of but little importance whether it is in anywise historical. For its value consists in the lessons which it inculcates, and the duties which it prescribes to those who receive it. The parables and allegories of the Scriptures are not less valuable than history. Nay, they are more so, because ancient history is little instructive, and truths are concealed in and symbolized by the legend and the Myth." (Morals and Dogma, p. 210.)

We should bear this fact in mind when we consider the degrees of the Scottish Rite, especially that of the Rose Croix. The legend upon which this degree is based is purely symbolical, and as such conveys a grand truth. Some, however, have thought that the

doctrine of this degree excluded the non-Christian, which shows how the purpose of Masonry has been misunderstood.

Gen. Pike, in speaking of the degree, says, "No Mason has the right to interpret the symbols of this degree for another, or to refuse him its mysteries, if he will not take them with the explanation and commentary superadded." Again he says, "Each of us makes such applications to his own faith and creed of the symbols and ceremonies of this degree, as seems to him proper." (Morals and Dogma, Ch. XVIII.) This is well said. Every intelligent Mason should make a protest against the crude and antiquated explanations of the symbols given in this degree. The degree itself is not necessarily sectarian, but the explanations adopted in the work are not only sectarian and un-Masonic, but they belong to a system of things which intelligent people are fast leaving behind.

Let me briefly summarize the explanation given by the authority just quoted. The cross has been a sacred symbol from the earliest antiquity. It is found upon all the enduring monuments of the world, in Egypt, Assyria, India, Persia, Mexico, etc. Its peculiar meaning in this degree is that given to it by the ancient Egyptian Thoth or Phtha, who is represented on the oldest monuments carrying in his hand the Crux Ansata,-- a tau cross with a ring over it. This was the hieroglyph for life, and with a triangle prefixed meant life-giving. To us, therefore, it is the symbol of life,--of that life that emanates from Deity and of that Eternal life for which we hope. The Rose was anciently sacred to Aurora and the Sun. It is a symbol of dawn, of the resurrection, Light, and the renewal of Life. The Cross and Rose together signify hieroglyphically, the Dawn of Eternal Life and the advent of a Saviour for which all nations hope. To the letters "I. N. R. I." Inscribed on the Crux Ansata, many meanings have been assigned. The Christian sees in them the initials of the inscription upon the Cross of Christ-- IESUE NAZAREMUS REX IUDEORUM. The Sages of antiquity connected it with one of the greatest secrets of nature, that of universal regeneration. They interpreted it thus: IGNE NATURA RENOVATUR INTEGRA--Nature is renovated by fire. The Alchemists and Hermetic Masons framed for it this aphorism, IGNE NITRUM RORIS INVENITUR. The letters are initials of the Hebrew words that represent the four elements--IAMMIM, the sea or water; NOUR, fire; ROUACE, the air; IEBESCHAH, the earth. (Ibid, Ch. XVIII.)

This degree symbolized the final triumph of truth over falsehood, of life over death, of good over evil. "No one Mason has a right to measure for another within the walls of a Masonic Temple, the degree of veneration which he shall feel for any Reformer, or Founder of any Religion. We teach a belief in no particular creed as we teach unbelief in none." (Ibid, p. 308.) But we recognize in the Founder of the Christian religion, an Initiate into the True Mysteries; one who came to rebuild again the eternal verities, to utter again the Divine Wisdom to a needy world. The Knight of the Rose Croix will revere his memory, and honour him as one of the true servants of the Most High. We recognize all Initiates as Brothers. We belong to no creed. We invite men of all religions to enlist under our banner and work to bring in a better day.

Dr. Mackey says, "If Masonry were simply a Christian institution,

the Jew and the Moslem, the Brahmin and the Buddhist, could not conscientiously partake of its illumination; but its universality is its boast. In its language citizens of every nation may converse; at its altar men of all religions may kneel; to its creed disciples of every faith may subscribe." (The Symbolism of Freemasonry, Mackey, p. 237.)

We have dwelt upon this degree because of the principle involved. The legends upon which this degree is based, while drawn from the New Testament, are also to be found in many other world Scriptures, for the symbolism, of which the real meaning has been shown in earlier lectures, is universal. The degree itself is really out of place in the Scottish Rite system; it should belong in the Templar system, if anywhere.

To again quote Gen. Pike, "We teach the truth of none of the legends we recite. They are to us but parables and allegories, involving and enveloping Masonic instruction; the vehicles of useful and interest information. . . Every one being at liberty to apply our symbols and emblems as he thinks most consistent with truth and reason and with his own faith." (Morals and Dogma, p.

329. ) Let every Scottish Rite Mason bear this fact in mind; and it would be well for the Knight Templar to remember this also, for there we have the same symbols and the same crude interpretation of them. These symbols, as we have seen, refer to realities in the divine life of Jesus, rather than to the incidents in his physical experiences.

In the early days of the Scottish Rite the system was full of grotesque and incongruous things, of contradictions and fantastic extravagances. The Supreme Council of the Southern Jurisdiction of the United States at length undertook the task of revising the work of the thirty degrees under its jurisdiction, but while this was done with considerable success there are still anachronisms and contradictions which should be eliminated to make the system harmonious.

The moral teaching of all the Rites is excellent. One who lives up to the standard inculcated in the Scottish Rite degrees will fulfil every demand made by the strictest code of morality.

## 11

## LECTURE X

THE SYMBOLS AND LEGENDS OF MASONRY. The real secrets of Masonry lie concealed in its symbols and legends.

These symbols and legends are the means by which the divine truths of Masonry are conveyed to the neophyte. This was the method of instruction in the Ancient Mysteries, and it was naturally adopted in the institution of Freemasonry. "To form symbols and to interpret them," says Creuzer, "were the main occupations of the ancient priesthood," and the myths were invented to illustrate a philosophic or religious truth.

Dr. Mackey, after discussing the question of myths, says, "It must be evident, from all that has been said respecting the analogy in origin and design between the Masonic and the ancient religious myths, that no one acquainted with the true science of this subject can, for a moment, contend that all the legends and traditions of the order are, to the very letter, historical facts." (Symbolism of Freemasonry, Mackey, p. 207.) He gives as an illustration of this the myth of the Winding Stairs, which, he says, "taken in its literal sense, is, in all its parts, opposed to history and probability."

Again, he calls attention to the myth which traces the origin of Freemasonry to the beginning of the world, "A myth, which is," he says, "even to this day, ignorantly interpreted, by some, as an historical fact, and the reference to which is still preserved in the date of 'anno lucis,' which is affixed to all masonic documents." This he calls a "philosophical myth, symbolizing the idea which analogically connects the creation of physical light in the universe with the birth of masonic or spiritual and intellectual light in the candidate. The one is; the type of the other." (Ibid, p. 211.) In the legends of the Master's Degree and of the Royal Arch he points out that there is a commingling of the historical myth and the mythical history so that much care must be taken in discriminating between the different elements.

Dr. Mackey then sums up the duty of a Mason as follows, "He who desires properly to appreciate the profound wisdom of the institution of which he is the disciple, must not be content, with uninquiring credulity, to accept all the traditions that are imparted to him as veritable histories; nor yet, with unphilosophic incredulity, to reject them in a mass, as fabulous inventions. In these extremes there is equal error. 'The myth,' says Hermann, 'is the representation of an idea.' It is for that idea that the student must search in the myths of Masonry. Beneath every one of them there is something richer and more spiritual than the mere narrative. . . Every one, therefore, who desires to be a skillful Mason, must not suppose that the task is accomplished by a perfect knowledge of the mere phraseology of the ritual, by a readiness in opening and closing a lodge, nor by an off-hand capacity to confer degrees. All these are good in their places, but without the internal meaning they are but mere child's play. He must study the myths, the traditions, and the symbols of the order, and learn their true interpretation; for this alone constitutes the science and the philosophy--the end, aim, and design of Speculative Masonry." (Ibid, p. 212, 214.)

These deeper things, as Dr. Mackey intimates, are not found in the monitorial explanations. J. D. Buck a 32nd degree Mason, in his wonderful book on Mystic Masonry, says, "The most profound secrets of Masonry are not revealed in the Lodge at all. They belong only to the few. . . But these secrets must be sought by the individual himself, and the candidate is debarred from possessing them solely by his own inattention to the hints everywhere given in the ritual of the Lodge, or by his indifference to the subject. If he, prefers to treat the whole subject with contempt, and to deny that any such real knowledge exists, it becomes evident that he not only closes the door against the possibility of himself possessing such

knowledge, but he also becomes impervious to any evidence of its existence that might come to him at any time. He has no one but himself to blame if he is left in darkness." (Mystic Masonry, Buck, p. XXXVI.)
The ritual and monitorial lessons of the Lodge teach nothing new, and the explanations of the symbols are often puerile and inadequate. Gen. Pike says, "There is no sight under the sun more pitiful and ludicrous at once, than the spectacle of the Prestons and the Webbs, not to mention the later incarnations of Dullness and Commoplace, undertaking to 'explain' the old symbols of Masonry, and adding to and 'improving' them, or inventing new ones. To the Circle enclosing the central point, and itself traced between two parallel lines, a figure purely Kabbalistic; these persons have added the super-imposed Bible, and even reared on that the ladder with three or nine rounds and then given a vapid interpretation of the whole, so profoundly absurd as actually to excite admiration." (Morals and Dogma, Pike, p. 105.)

The exegesis is also often crude. This is not strange, as the ritual was written before the days of modern Biblical scholarship, and perhaps it would be well if the ritual were revised. These immature conceptions could be eliminated without affecting the meaning and beauty of the ceremonies. However, if we bear in mind that Masonry does not indorse its legends as literal facts, no harm can be done.
We will now consider some of the symbols and myths of the Fraternity.
THE LODGE.
The Lodge represents King Solomon's Temple. The temple is a symbolic image of the universe, and as such is symbolic in all its parts and arrangements, therefore, the temple of Solomon resembles all the temples of antiquity that practiced the Mysteries.
The Hebrews, like other peoples, made much of the system of numbers

to convey their hidden meaning. The Holy of Holies formed a cube, corresponding to the number four, which represents manifested nature, while the three sides or faces of the figure, when drawn on a plane surface, represented the Deity, the three aspects of Will, Wisdom and Activity (Intelligence). Everything within the temple was symbolically arranged. The ceiling, supported by twelve columns, represented the twelve months of the year; the borders around the columns and the candlestick with the twelve lights represented the twelve signs of the zodiac; the seven lights, the seven planets; the veils of four colors represented the four elements, etc. In the Royal Arch Degree of the American Rite, the Tabernacle has four veils of different colors, to each of which belongs a banner and on each banner is inscribed one of the four images; the Bull, the Lion, the Man, the Eagle. These constellations answered to the equatorial and solstitial points of 2500 years B.C. The four signs Taurus, Leo, Scorpio, and Aquarius, were termed the fixed signs, and are assigned to the four veils.

The Sun entered Taurus at the vernal equinox, Leo at the Summer solstice, Scorpio at the autumnal equinox (for which, on account of

its malignant influence, Aquilla, the eagle was substituted), and Aquarius at the winter solstice.

Every temple was a representation of the universe, and in them the great lights of Nature played an important part. The images of the Sun, Moon, and Mercury were represented, and even in our Lodge rooms they constitute the three lights, except that for Mercury the Master of the Lodge has been substituted. Eusebius tells us that the officers of the Eleusinian Mysteries were the Hierophant, representing the Great Architect of the Universe; the torch-bearer, representing the Sun; the altar-bearer, representing the Moon; and the sacred herald, representing Mercury. The latter was charged with excluding the profane from the Mysteries.

Every Lodge, as we have said, represents the Temple. The two great columns between which you pass as you enter the Lodge represent the two great pillars, 30 feet 8 inches high; 6 feet 10 inches in diameter, which stood in the porch of the temple on either side of the Eastern gateway. These columns represent the two pillars of Hercules,--the solstices, Capricorn and Cancer, the two gates of heaven,--and were imitations by the Tyrian artist of the columns at the entrance of the temple of Malkarth in Tyre.

The Lodge is said to be due east and west as King Solomon's Temple was so situated. All the temples of Antiquity were usually thus built. Pythagoras also arranged his assemblies due east and west because he held that motion began in the east and proceeded west. The Egyptian and Mexican Pyramids were also built to the four cardinal points of the compass, while beneath the Temple, extending east and west, was a subterranean cavern used for Initiation. No well equipped Lodge is lacking in this particular.

THE FURNISHING OF THE LODGE.

The Holy Bible, Square and Compasses, together with a Charter or Dispensation, constitute the furnishings of the Lodge.

(1)   The Holy Bible. This in a Christian Lodge consists of the Old and New Testaments; a Hebrew Lodge would use the Old Testament only; a Mohammedan Lodge, the Koran; in like manner a Buddhist Lodge could use the Tripitaka, a Hindu Lodge the Vedas, etc. The obligation of the candidate is always taken on the Sacred Book of his religion, for his Holy Bible is his Light, in accordance with which he should live and walk.

(2)   The Square and Compasses. These symbols are perhaps the most familiar to the general public of any in Masonry. I need not dwell on the lessons in morality which the square and compasses teach. Masonry is, however, something more than a system of morality, and it is this inner significance that I have endeavoured to set forth.

There is a science and philosophy concealed in these symbols which Dr. Buck explains as follows: "The Square with its one right angle and its scale of measurements applies to surfaces and solids, and deals with the apparently fixed states of matter. It represents solidarity, symmetry and proportion; and this involves the sciences of arithmetic and geometry. The Compasses with moveable angle set

in the Lodge at an angle of 60 degrees, applies to the circle and the sphere; to movements and revolutions. In a general sense, the square is a symbol of matter and the earth, the Compasses of Spirit and the heavens." (Mystic Masonry, Buck, p. 242.)

The position of the Square and Compasses indicates the progress of the candidate from Entered Apprentice to-that of Master Mason.

THE ORNAMENTS.

The Ornaments of a Lodge are the Mosaic Pavement, the Indented Tessel, and the Blazing Star.

The Mosaic Pavement is supposed to represent the ground floor of King Solomon's Temple; the Indented Tessel, the border or skirting surrounding it. There is no evidence that either existed in the ancient temple, but the symbol is significant as it denotes the checkered course of life, also the two opposing principles in Nature,--Light and Darkness, Michael and Satan, Balder and Loki, Ormuzd and Ahriman, etc.

The Blazing Star also represents these two principles. If the point is turned upward it represents God, Good, Order, or the Lamb of Ormuzd and St. John; if the point is turned downward it denotes Lucifer, Evil, Disorder, or the accursed Goat of Mendes and the Mysteries. The Blazing Star or Pentagram also represents the human body,--the five points representing the four limbs and head. It is thus called the sign of the Microcosm. All the Mysteries of Magic were said to be summed up in this symbol. Paracelsus pronounces it the greatest and most potent of all signs.

THE ALL SEEING EYE.

This symbol, in the Ancient Mysteries, indicated the sight that annuls time and space. This is the symbol of the higher clairvoyance. The Master always possessed this sight. In India this All Seeing Eye was called the Eye of Siva. The Egyptians represented Osiris by the symbol of an open eye, and placed this hieroglyphic of him in all their temples. In the

Lodge the All Seeing Eye represents the Omniscience of God, --The Eye that never sleeps. It may also represent, as in the Ancient Mysteries, the higher vision.

THE LETTER G.

This letter is the natural symbol among English speaking people for God. It is a substitute in American Lodges for the Hebrew Yod, which is the Kabbalistic symbol for unity. In France the letter Yod is put in the Blazing Star.

THE CLASPED HANDS.

This symbol was used by Pythagoras and represented the sacred number ten--the number expressed by the mysterious Tetractys. This figure was represented in the form of the triangle. The Hebrews formed it with the letters of the Divine Name. Both Pythagoras and the Hebrew priests borrowed the figure from the sacred science of

Egypt.

THE TRIANGLE AND DOUBLE TRIANGLE.

All the nations of antiquity considered the triangle as sacred. It was one of the most common symbols for the Deity. The three sides typify the three aspects of God--Will, Wisdom and Intelligence.

Here we have the Trinity in Unity.

The double triangle interlaced, symbolizes the manifested universe--the union of spirit and matter. The triangle pointing upward is spirit or fire; the one pointing downward is matter or water. One represents the descent of spirit into matter, the other the ascent of matter to spirit. The union of the two, in the manifested universe, is inseparable. This double triangle is used in India to symbolize two Hindu Gods, or rather the two aspects of Ishvara-- Siva and Vishnu. It also represents the six points, the senary, which with the point in the center is the septinary.

THE LIGHT.

There are three greater and three lesser lights in Masonry, and though the ritual does not give any explanation of these symbols, there is an important meaning connected with them. The Sun is an ancient symbol of the Logos--it signifies the male aspect, the life-giving and generative power. God is the source of light, and light is the cause of life. The Moon represents the passive, or female aspect of Nature.

JACOB'S LADDER.

The mystical ladder which Jacob in his vision saw, extending from earth to heaven, was a common symbol in the Ancient Mysteries, and was always composed of seven steps or rounds. The ladder symbolized the progress of man from his present to higher conditions--each round representing one of the seven stages of his evolutionary progress. In the Mysteries of Persia and India this mystic ladder was an important symbol, especially in the former, where a ladder of seven rounds was erected in each of their temples.

The seven steps also correspond to the seven gates through which the candidate was passed successively in his journeyings through the seven caverns of Initiation, and symbolized the seven conditions or subplanes of Hades. The seven steps, seven gates, seven halls, seven worlds, seven planes, etc., are all symbols~ of the various stages of the soul's progress. The ancient Initiates held that the evolution of the human soul took place through a series of seven globes situated on the three lower planes of the universe. The life wave passes seven times round this world chain, and through seven stages on each globe. The progress involves a downward and an upward arc-- a descent of spirit into matter and a re-ascent of spirit to God. This is symbolized in Jacob's vision by the angels ascending and descending.

Jacob's ladder is sometimes misrepresented with three or nine

rounds; it should have seven. Dr. Mackey says that "The error arose from the ignorance of those inventors who first engraved the masonic symbols for our monitors. The ladder of Masonry, like the equipollent ladders of its kindred institutions, always had seven steps, although in modern times the three principal or upper ones are alone alluded to. These rounds, beginning at the lowest, are Temperance, Fortitude, Prudence, Justice, Faith, Hope, and Charity." ( The Symbolism of Freemasonry, Mackey, p. 120.) The application of these virtues, however, is a later addition to symbolism.

The seven rounds are also emblematical of the seven planes of the universe--physical, astral, mental buddhic, atmic, anupadika and adi; the seven ancient elements earth, water, fire, air, ether, and two unnamed; the seven subplanes of the astral world-- astral solid, liquid, gaseous, etheric, super-etheric, sub atomic, and atomic; the seven metals--lead, quicksilver, copper, tin, iron, silver, and gold; the seven colors--black, purple, green, blue, red, white, and yellow; the seven stones--diamond, amethyst, emerald, sapphire, ruby, pearl, and topaz; the seven ancient planets--Saturn, Mercury, Venus, Jupiter, Mars, Luna and Sol. Thus the seven-stepped ladder had various applications and correspondences, Its presence in the Masonic institutions is evidence of the close analogy between Freemasonry and the Ancient Mysteries.

## THE RIGHT ANGLED TRIANGLE, OR THE 47TH PROBLEM OF EUCLID.

This is one of the most important symbols of antiquity. The perpendicular line, whose measurement is 3, represents the active, male principle; the base line, whose measurement is 4, represents the passive, female principle; and their union, or the addition of the squares of these numbers, will produce a square whose root will be the hypotheneuse,--a line measured by 5 and representing the universe. The square of the perpendicular and base, $9 + 16 = 25$, the square root of which is 5, the number of the hypotheneuse. It was taught in all the Mysteries that the union of the male and female principles of Nature produced the universe. This is the occult meaning of the 47th problem of Euclid--the sum of the squares of the perpendicular and base of a right angle triangle equals the square of the hypotheneuse. This is a symbol of perfect proportion between number and forms; between spirit and matter.

The three sides of the triangle bear the proportions, as we have seen, of 3, 4, and 5, and $32 + 43 = 52$, or $9 + 16 = 25$; also $9 + 16 + 25 = 50$. Thus the number 50 is based on the proportion of the sides of the right angled triangle.

Philo speaks of two series, which he calls triangles and squares; namely, 1, 3, 6, 10 and 1, 4, 9, 16. With regard to the triangle series 1, 3, 6, 10, it is interesting to note that $1 = 1$; $3 = 1 + 2$; $6 = 1 + 2 + 3$; and $10 = 1 + 2 + 3 + 4$. In the square series, 1, 4, 9, 16; $1 = 1^2$; $4 = 2^2$; $9 = 3^2$; and $16 = 4^2$; $1 + 3 + 6 + 10 = 20$; and $1 + 4 + 9 + 16 = 30$; and $20 + 30 = 50$; 50 was a sacred number, and was derived from the right angled triangle. The greatest Jewish festival (Jubilee) took place every fifty years.

## THE LAMB-SKIN OR WHITE LEATHER APRON.

In the Ancient Mysteries the investiture of the Apron formed an essential part of the ceremony of Initiation. The Apron and White Robe were symbols of purity. In Persia the investiture was exceedingly imposing. The candidate having taken the oath of secrecy, was given the insignia of the Order--the Girdle, the Tiara, the White Apron and the Purple Tunic. The Japanese candidate was also clothed in certain Garments which consisted of a Loose Tunic and White Apron bound round the loins with a girdle. In the degree of holiness practiced by the Pharisees the "noviciate" was also given an Apron as a symbol of purity. The Essenes and Druids invested their candidates with a White Robe, and the Scandinavians gave the candidate a White Shield. In all these ceremonies whatever the material or form, the symbolic significance was always the same. The White Apron of Masonry was derived from these ancient ceremonies, and is one of the most significant symbols in our Order; the color "White" having been an emblem of Light and Purity from time immemorial.

The shape and combination of the Masonic Apron is that of a triangle overlapping a square, representing the occult septenary nature of man. The triangle symbolizes spirit, or the three highest principles; the square or quaternary the four lowest. Each principle is correlated to a plane, a round and a race. The spiritual triad is the spiritual body of St. Paul, and the quaternary the natural body. The triad, which is the immortal part of man, contains potentially all the powers of Divinity; and to develop these latent attributes it must descend into matter--the triangle must incarnate in the square. This is represented in Masonry by the degree of Entered Apprentice, and is symbolized by the way in which the Apprentice is taught to wear his Apron. The spiritual is subordinate to the material earthly desires and passions rule supreme. But the candidate is here to learn to subdue his passions; his partial success is represented by the degree of Fellow Craft, and is symbolized by the way he wears his Apron in that degree. The complete triumph of the spiritual is represented by the Master Mason degree, and is again indicated by the Apron.

This state was represented in the Ancient Mysteries by the mystical death and resurrection of the candidate. The perfected Initiate has mastered his lower nature and has become the Perfect Man,--Hermes, Buddha, or Christ.

The symbolism of the Apron is indeed far reaching.

Let every Mason remember how he impersonated the Grand Master. He should never forget its deep significance. In the Ancient Mysteries the candidate did not merely impersonate the Master, he himself became the Master--the ceremony merely symbolizing what he became. It is a mistake to suppose, as some writers have, that the candidate in the mystic rites was merely representing the events connected with the tragedy of the Master or God from whom the Mysteries derived their name. The story of the Master or God was wholly an allegory of the experiences of the Initiate, while the rites were but typical of the various stages in the growth of the soul. In the process of becoming a Christ he represents all those who have attained the Christ state, for all masters have passed

through the experiences symbolized by the Myth.

Masonry has a truer conception than any exoteric religion, for these religions take the symbol for the thing symbolized, but Masonry, in making the candidate impersonate Hiram, has preserved the original teaching. Hiram is identical with the Sun-Gods of all nations--it is a universal glyph, for all real Initiation is an internal process, a regeneration, the consummation of which is the Perfect Man or Master, the goal of human evolution.

In the Ancient Mysteries there was a further Rite which symbolized the next stage, that of union with the Divine, the At-One-Ment.

This was the Ascension, and is symbolized by the square enclosed in the triangle. - The lower nature is here refined and "ascends to the Father." God is All in All.

As we have already said, each principle in man's constitution is correlated to a plane. A knowledge of these planes would enable a man by a trained will to direct the forces on each plane. Such is the power of a real Master.

## 12

# LECTURE XI

THE SYMBOLS AND LEGENDS OF MASONRY (Continued.)

In this concluding lecture of the series, we will consider the remaining important symbols and legends of Masonry.

## SACRED OR INEFFABLE NAME.

This symbol was universal in ancient times, for every nation of antiquity had its Sacred Name or Ineffable Word. The Hebrew symbol consists of four letters, Yod, He, Vau, He, and is called the Tetragrammaton, or four lettered word. This word was said to have been communicated by God to Moses at the burning bush. The name was held most sacred by the Jews, but its meaning and proper pronunciation has long been obscured.

Before the invention of the masoretic points the pronunciation of a word in the Hebrew language could not be known by the characters themselves, so it was easy in the course of time to lose the proper pronunciation. Especially so, as at the beginning of the Hellenistic age the use of the name was reserved for the temple. At the beginning of the Christian era, Philo writes, "The four letters may be mentioned or heard only by holy men whose ears and tongues are prepared by wisdom, and by no others in any place whatsoever." In the course of time the pronunciation of the name, even by the temple priests, fell into disuse, and the manner of its pronunciation at length became a secret entrusted only to the few. While the word was being withdrawn from common use, it was pronounced "Adonai" in the scriptures, and when the vowel points were introduced those that belonged to Adonai were placed under the Tetra-grammaton.

The word itself is a symbol; the letters are probably arranged as a blind. As they stand in the Tetragrammaton they have no significance. They do not represent any real Hebrew word. Now if we apply the Hebrew method of halving or transposing letters which was used to conceal the meaning of a word, or rather if we reverse the process which may have been employed, we get instead of Y. H. V. H., H. V. H. Y. Before the introduction of vowel signs, certain weak consonants such as Yod and Vau, were sometimes used to indicate vowel sounds, so we frequently see I or E given as an equivalent for Yod, and U or O given for Vau. Even Yod is sometimes given as Jod, and Vau as Waw, so we have the name given as Y. H. V.
H. or I. H. V. H. or J. H. V. H., or Y. H. W. H., or I.H.O.H.,etc.
Now the personal pronouns He and She are written in Hebrew with the signs He, Vau, A-leph, and He, Yod, A-leph. When A-leph terminates a word, and has no vowel immediately preceding or following, it is usually dropped. Now if we drop the final A-leph we have the transposed Tetra-grammaton, H. V. H. Y., which are the personal pronouns He and She, the male and female, representing the two great principles of nature,-- the dual aspect of the Second Logos.
Now if we turn to the Kabbalah, which contains some portions of the secret teachings of the Jews, we shall find that this great principle is the exact meaning of the Tetragrammaton. It does not represent the Ab-solute Deity, or the Unmanifested Logos, but it does represent the man-ifested, the first emanation--Adam Kadmon.
The two aspects of Being which are potential in the First Logos, become manifested in the later stages of evolution. This name represents the four worlds--Alseluth, signified by Yod, Briah by He, Yezerah by Vau, and Asiah by the Second He. The source of the Tetragrammaton is Ab-solute Deity, Ain-Soph, the Causeless Cause. The Tetragrammaton is also the Sephiroth, which are ten in number, and emanate one from the

other. The highest is Kether,-the Crown; then comes Chockmah and Binah, the male and female principles. From these emanate the other seven. The very fact that the meaning of the Tetragrammaton is identical with the words obtained by transposing the letters, is sufficient evidence that the word was really H. V. (or W. U. O.) H. Y. (or J. I. E.), according to the equivalents adopted for the signs--whether interpreted as consonants or vowels--and the names given to the signs.

The meaning and pronunciation of the word was carefully guarded. There is no hint given in the ritual for this secrecy, but there is a scientific reason, for the mystic Word has to do with the science of rhythmic vibrations which is the key to the equilibrium of all forces. In all mysticism the knowledge of names meant the possession of powers. The spoken name gave one the power of the name. It is interesting to note how the Jews worked this idea into their system. In the Talmud the wonderful works of Jesus are ascribed to his use of the Sacred Name. According to early traditions the knowledge whereby he wrought these works was learned in Egypt, but in the developed Toldoth the "word of power" was the Holy Name,--the Tetgrammaton.

All nations of antiquity had their Sacred Flames, which were "Words of Power." These names were formed by taking a letter which conveyed a meaning and adding other letters each having a meaning;

the whole word thus formed constituting a Sacred Name or Word, which contains some great truth. These Names were Words of Power, for, as the unfolding consciousness realizes one truth after another and becomes that truth, it rules. In Persia the Sacred Name was H. O. M., in India A. U. M., in Scandinavia I. O. W., in Greece I. A. O., etc.

THE RITE OF CIRCUMAMBULATION.

This Rite again connects Freemasonry with the Ancient Mysteries. It consists in a formal procession around the altar, and originally alluded to the apparent course of the sun which is from east to west. In ancient Greece the priests, during the Rites of sacrifice, walked three times around the altar while chanting a sacred hymn, which was divided into three parts, and each part was to be sung at a particular point in the procession. The analogy between this practice of the ancients and the recitations of a passage of Scripture in the Masonic circumambulation is quite apparent. In making this circuit it was considered necessary that the right side should always be next to the altar, and so the procession moved from west to the north, then east, south, west and then to the north again. We find the same Rite among the Romans, Druids, and Hindus. In all these ceremonies they were "imitating the example of the sun and following his beneficent course."

THE LEGEND OF THE WINDING STAIRS.

This Legend is connected with the Fellow Craft degree. It is based upon I Kings, vi, 8, "The door for the middle chamber was in the right side of the house; and they went up with winding stairs into the middle chamber, and out of the middle into the third."

"Out of this slender material," says Dr. Mackey, "has been constructed an allegory, which, if properly considered in its symbolical relations, will be found to be of surpassing beauty. But it is only as a symbol that we can regard this whole tradition; for the historical facts and the architectural details alike forbid us for a moment to suppose that the legend, as it is rehearsed in the second degree of Masonry, is anything more than a magnificent philosophical myth." (The Symbolism of Freemasonry, Mackey, p.

215.)

The lesson which this legend teaches is not difficult to discover. Freemasonry is a speculative science which has for its object the investigation of divine truth. The candidate is in search of more light, and as all the ceremonies denote a progress from a lower to a higher state, he is always progressing. This fundamental symbolism of Masonry is found in each degree. There is the mystical ladder, the ceremony of circumambulation, the restoration to life, etc. The Legend of the Winding Stairs symbolizes the same fact--the ascent of man from ignorance to knowledge, from darkness to light, from death to life.

The steps of the Winding Stairs commenced on the porch of the Temple. This indicates the beginning of the masonic life--the preparation for entering the temple.

It is curious to note that the number of steps in all the systems has been odd. This probably is due to the fact that the symbolism of numbers was borrowed from Pythagoras, in whose system of philosophy the odd numbers were regarded as sacred, though the number of steps has greatly varied. Tracing boards have been found in which only five steps are represented, and others which denote seven. At one time in England the number was thirty-eight, which was reduced to thirty-seven, and in this country the number has been reduced to fifteen. Perhaps five would be the more appropriate as the stairs only extended to the middle chamber. The number seven, corresponding to the number of rounds in the mystic ladder, would indicate the attainment of perfection-- the Holy of Holies.

We might say that the complete stairs are composed of seven steps,--three carrying the candidate into the ground floor of the temple, two into the middle, and two into the inner sanctuary The general symbolism of the Legend is not affected by the number of steps, or the method of division.

The candidate who succeeds in climbing the Winding Stairs will receive his reward. What is the reward or wages of the Speculative Mason? Not silver nor gold, but Truth. Yet the whole of divine truth cannot be imparted to the Fellow Craft. The Middle Chamber, then, where he receives his wages, is symbolical of the Fellow Craft degree, and the wages are appropriate to the degree of his progress.

To again quote Dr. Mackey, "It is, then, as a symbol, and a symbol only, that we must study this beautiful legend of the Winding Stairs. If we attempt to adopt it as an historical fact, the absurdity of its details stares us in the face, and wise men will wonder at our credulity. Its inventors had no desire thus to impose upon our folly; but offering it to us as a great philosophical myth, they did not for a moment suppose that we would pass over its sublime moral teachings to accept the allegory as an historical narrative, without meaning, and wholly irreconcilable with the records of Scripture, and opposed by all the principles of probability. To suppose that eighty thousand craftsmen were weekly paid in the narrow precincts of the temple chambers, is simply to suppose an absurdity." (Ibid, p. 226.)

We must guard against the materialization of our allegories and symbols. Remember Masonry is a "system of morality, veiled in allegory and illustrated by symbols." To regard the myths as history is to miss the truth which the symbols were designed to teach. No intelligent Mason will fall into this error.

## THE HIRAM LEGEND AND THE MASTER'S DEGREE.

The Hiram Legend and the Master's Degree are derived from the Mysteries. They are the latest expression of the old Sun Myth and the Ancient Rite.

Dr. Mackey, in speaking of the symbol of Hiram, says, "It was evidently borrowed from the pagan Mysteries, where Bacchus, Adonis, Proserpina, and a host of other apotheosized beings play the same role that Hiram does in the Masonic Mysteries." (Ibid, p. 20.)

I have given various forms of these Legends--the Osiris, Atys, Hu, Balder, and others. In each of them the Hero of the Myth dies or is deprived of life, is laid away in the tomb, and rises again œrom the grave. This ceremony was called the mystical death and resurrection.

The legend represents the activity of the Logos in the cosmos, and the mystic life of the Initiate. The ancient legends and symbols always have a double meaning and sometimes more. The lectures on True Initiation set forth in detail the two aspects of the Sun Myth--the mythic and the mystic. To the uninitiated' the cosmic or mythic aspect of the legend was the only one seen, thus the Rites were supposed by them merely to typify the death and resurrection of some Hero or Demi God, as Osiris, Mithra, Atys, Adonis, Tammuz, etc., and so the Sun was worshipped under these titles. Perhaps this was natural enough, for the visible Sun was a symbol not only of the Logos, the Spiritual Sun, but also of the Initiate. The yearly course of the Sun represented in one aspect the mystic life of the Initiate.

You will recall that in the Hindu Mysteries when the candidate reached the south in his circuits, he said, "I copy the example of the Sun, and follow his beneficent course." This example was not merely external. The Sun is a symbol of the Logos, and its yearly course typifies the work of the Logos, so that he candidate, by representing the Sun and following his course, is really following the example of the Logos;--the Sun Myth typifying both the activity of the Logos and the mystic life of the Initiate.

In the true Mysteries the Rites symbolized the various stages of this mystic life. Complete mastery over the lower nature was typified by placing the candidate in a trance and laying him away in a sepulcher for three days and nights. In the Pseudo Mysteries the aspirant was confined in a cell in his normal state, and kept there in fear and darkness that he might reflect on the seriousness of the step taken, and be better prepared to receive the mysterious truths bequeathed from the ancient days. This was the symbolical death, the deliverance from which was called the resurrection.

While confined in his cell the search for the Hero was made and his body finally found.

The Master Mason will here see the source of the Hiram Legend, and the Master's Degree. I am not permitted to say more, neither is it necessary for those who are qualified will understand. Mr. Singleton, 33rd degree, after describing the mystical death in the Ancient Mysteries, says, "The Intelligent Mason will, from this, discover the origin of the Rites in the 3rd Degree of Symbolic Masonry and the 5th and 31st Degrees, A. A. S. R.... The Mysteries, in: all their forms, were funereal. They celebrated the mystical death and revivification of some individual by the use of emblems, symbols, and allegorical representations." (History of Freemasonry and Concordant Orders, p. 73.) Mr. Singleton is here in error in regard to the purpose of the Mysteries, if he means that they merely celebrated the mystical death and resurrection of some one individual. The ceremonies of Initiation symbolized the progress of the human soul, and the mystical death and resurrection were experienced by every Initiate. Perhaps in the latter days of the

Mysteries, when no true Initiation took place, the ceremonies may have been considered as symbolizing the experiences of some special individual, but such was not the case in the true Mysteries.

We see thus that the story of Hiram is but a variation of the ancient and universal legend, in which Osiris, Adonis, Dionysus, Balder, Hu, and many more have played the principal part. Some call Hiram a "mythical symbol." This is true, but he is also a mystical symbol. Mythically Hiram is the Sun, a symbol of the Logos; mystically he is the perfect Initiate, the Grand Master. The myth was not intended to add to the facts of history, but, as De Witte points out, "to illustrate a philosophical or religious truth."

We must here utter a protest against the sectarian interpretation of the Master Mason's degree. It is true that the degree embraces the inner truths of Christianity, in common with all the mystic teaching. But the origin of the degree and all its symbols and legends were derived from the Ancient Mysteries, and to call the degree a Christian institution, as do Hutchinson and Oliver, is erroneous. Dr. Mackey, in speaking of this tendency to Christianize Masonry, says, "We find Christian Masonic writers indulging in it almost to an unwarrantable excess, and by the extent of their sectarian interpretations materially affecting the cosmopolitan character of the institution. This tendency to Christianization has, in some instances, been so universal, and has prevailed for so long a period, that certain symbols and myths have been, in this way, so deeply and thoroughly imbued with the Christian element as to leave those who have not penetrated into the cause of this peculiarity, in doubt whether they should attribute to the symbol an ancient or a modern and Christian origin. . . It is in this way that Masonry has, by a sort of inevitable process (when we look to the religious sentiment of the interpreters), been Christianized.

. . I do not object to the system when the interpretation is not strained.

. . all that I contend for is, that such interpretations are modern, and that they do not belong to, although they may often be deduced from, the ancient system." (The Symbolism of Freemasonry, Mackey, pp. 238, 246.)

THE SPRIG OF ACACIA.

In all the Ancient Mysteries there were sacred plants which were symbols of Initiation. The myrtle was used in the Mysteries of Greece, the areca in the Egyptian Mysteries, the mistletoe in the Druidical Mysteries, the lotus in the Indian Rites, the lettuce in the Mysteries of Adonis, etc. Masonry has borrowed this custom from the ancients and adopted the acacia, which was sacred among the Hebrews, as its mystic symbol.

The acacia was a sacred tree which grew abundantly in the vicinity of Jerusalem. The sanctuary of the tabernacle and the holy ark were constructed from this wood, and the tree ever afterwards was regarded as sacred.

This symbol has several meanings, but for our purpose we need mention only the primary and original meaning which is Initiation, and its use as a symbol of immortality and innocence. These are closely connected and must be considered together to get the full

meaning of the symbol. In olden days. Initiation was based upon innocence; that is, upon purity of life, and the Initiation brought a realization of immortality.

THE RITE OF DISCALCEATION.

This Rite refers to the act of uncovering the feet on approaching holy ground. It is a symbol of reverence, and was a common practice among all the nations of antiquity. The priests always offered sacrifices with uncovered feet. Pythagoras instructed his disciples to offer sacrifices and worship with their shoes off. The Mohammedans, when about to perform their devotions, always leave their slippers at the door of the Mosque. The Druids practiced the same custom whenever they celebrated the sacred rites. The Peruvians also left their shoes on the porch when they entered the temple. Dr. Oliver tells us that "The same usage prevailed equally in India, and the islands to the west of Europe; and even the American savages thought that uncovering the feet, while in the act of devotion, was a sublime method of paying honour to the Deity." (Signs and Symbols, Oliver, p. 153.)

The Jewish lawgivers adopted this sign of reverence, and the symbolism has descended to us. The application of the symbol to the third degree is well known to every Mason.

TEE STONE OF FOUNDATION.

This is the most important symbol of the Royal Arch degree. It must not be confounded with any of the other stone symbols, such as the corner-stone, the key-stone, or the cape-stone.

In the first place we need to understand that the symbol is purely allegorical. To accept it in a literal sense will present, as Dr. Mackey says, "Absurdities and puerilities which would not occur if the Stone of Foundation was received, as it really is, as a philosophical myth, conveying a most profound and beautiful symbolism. Read in this spirit, as all the legends of Masonry should be read, the mythical story of the Stone of Foundation becomes one of the most important and interesting of all the Masonic symbols." (The Symbolism of Freemasonry, p. 283.)

We have not time to trace the legendary history of the Stone of Foundation--probably more legends are connected with this stone than with any other Masonic symbol. The Masonic legends of the Stone of Foundation, like nearly all that are of Jewish origin, are derived from the Jewish Talmud, and owe their origin to the imaginative genius of the Talmudic writers. But there is this difference between Talmudists and Masons. The former accept all these traditions, with their puerilities, anachronisms, and absurdities, as historical, while the intelligent Mason receives them as allegories.

It would be interesting, did space permit, to give in full these Rabbinical reveries, and also the Masonic traditions based upon them. But I can only outline the tradition.

The Talmudic legends tell us that Enoch built a subterranean temple

on Mount Moriah, consisting of nine vaults situated beneath each other and communicating by apertures left in each vault. In the lowest arch he deposited a cubical stone, called afterwards the Stone of Foundation, on which had been inscribed the ineffiable name of God. He then made a door of stone, with a ring in it, and placed it over the opening of the uppermost arch, and covered it so that it could not be seen. In the destruction of the world by the deluge all trace of the subterranean temple was lost, but when David was digging for the foundation of the Temple, he discovered, in the lowest depths of the excavation, a certain stone on which the name of God was inscribed. This stone he removed and deposited in the Holy of Holies. It was a favourite theory of the Talmud legend makers that David laid the foundation upon which Solomon built the temple. The Masonic tradition is substantially the same as the Rabbinical, except that it substitutes Solomon for David as the discoverer of the stone, and makes him deposit it in the crypt of the temple, where it remained until the foundation of the second temple was laid, when it was discovered and placed in the Holy of Holies.

These legends, in the light of historical narratives, would be, as Lee says, "so many idle and absurd conceits," as facts, but as allegories they contain an important symbolism.

The symbolism and worship of stones in ancient times was almost universal. The Greeks originally used unhewn stones of a cubical form to represent their Gods. These consecrated stones were placed before the doors of the houses in Athens, also in front of the temples, in the schools and libraries, and at the corners of the streets.

The Thebans worshipped Bacchus under the form of a square stone: Arnobius says that Cybele was represented by a small stone of black color, and Eusebius cites Porphyry as saying that the ancients represented the Deity by a black stone because his nature was obscure and inscrutable. The Mohammedans also have a black stone, which was formerly worshipped and is still much reverenced by Musselmen. The

Druids represented their Gods by cubical stones, and we also find that the early American races worshipped square stones. These citations are taken from Mackey's "Symbolism of Freemasonry." They might easily be extended, but those given will suffice to show that everywhere in the ancient world cubical stones were used as a symbol of the Deity.

These mystical stones were all symbolic, and the legends connected with them allegories. The Masonic Stone and legend are no exceptions; the Stone of Foundation is but a symbol of the Deity.

THE LOST WORD.

The symbol of the Lost Word and the legend of the search for it, embodies the whole design of Freemasonry. The primary object of Freemasonry is the search after Divine Truth. The Word is a symbol of this Divine Truth, and this truth is the key to the "Science of the Soul." The real Master, then, is one learned in the Divine Science--a "Moses" to lead the neophyte through a wilderness of experience, from his ignorant self to a knowledge of his true Self,

a conscious union with God.

The symbolism of the Lost Word may be applied to the degradation of the Ancient Mysteries which resulted in the loss of the real Word-- the knowledge of occult science. From that time to this, men have ever been in search of the real Word, and although but few have been able to regain the knowledge of the true Mysteries, others have often caught glimpses of the inner meaning, which is symbolized by the Substituted Word. That the symbolism is not well understood is evident from the fact that but few Masons, if any,

to-day possess the knowledge and power implied in the symbols and legends of the Order; for this reason only "The Substitute"-- monitorial explanation--"is given to the neophyte until he, perhaps in future generations, shall find the True Word."

That Masonry was in search of the meaning of this symbolic Word, is clearly proven by the insight of the Revisionists in 1717, and the fact that Symbolic Masonry did not pretend to give the candidate the Lost

Word. They knew that the Word was no mere name, but a knowledge of occult science which could only be attained by soul development. Real Mastership must again be realized before the Lost Word can be found, and such realization must of necessity be the experience of each individual brother by whom it is found.

The use made of the tradition of the recovery of the Lost Word, and its impartation in the Royal Arch degree, shows that the later degree makers little realized the meaning of the symbolism. They mistook the symbol for the thing symbolized. The Royal Arch degree can only give the symbol. The real Word, which holds the inner meaning and the power of the symbol, is still a mystery. To understand this mystic symbol, and all that it implies, is to possess the key to the science of sciences-- the real Knowledge or Word of Power.

# CONCLUSION

We will now bring this series of lectures to a close. We have seen that Masonry is modeled on the Ancient Mysteries, and derives its important symbols and legends from that source. Is this a mere coincidence? Was there meant to be only a similarity in outward form? We cannot so believe; the analogy is far to close. The men who formulated the ritual very well knew what they were doing. We believe that the secret vaults contain jewels not yet discovered, and it should be the work of every true Mason to search diligently for "More Light." To discover the full meaning of the glyphs and allegories is to revive the Ancient Wisdom, the Secret Doctrine of Antiquity, the real Lost Word. That such Wisdom once existed will not be denied by any intelligent Mason, for the whole superstructure of the Order is based upon the traditions of its existence. Dr. Buck says, "Instead of being an imitation of the Mysteries of Antiquity, Masonry should become their Restoration and Perpetuation through the coming centuries, not by relaxing its discipline, or changing its ritual, but by deepening the learning, intensifying the zeal and elevating the aim of every Brother throughout the world." (Mystic Masonry, Buck, p. 79.)

We have seen that the Masters of old were true Occultists--Masters

of Divine Science. Masonry has preserved for us the names that indicate the reality of occult knowledge and power in the Perfect and Sublime Master, Prince Adept, Sublime Prince of the Royal Secret, etc. If these names do not imply that I have suggested they are a mere farce and should be abolished. That they are empty titles to-day all will agree; many having recognized this fact, are calling for their abolition. But I hold that instead of abolishing the titles we should endeavour to make them stand, in fact, for what in name the indicate. This would be in line with the ancient tradition--a recovery of the real Lost Word, the key to the Science of Knowledge. Every Mason should labour assiduously for the realization of this ideal. Let us not be content with the mere rudiments of our philosophy. "That skill," says Dr. Mackey, "which consists in repeating with fluency and precision, the ordinary lectures, in complying with all the ceremonial requisitions of the ritual, or the giving, with sufficient accuracy, the appointed modes of recognition, pertains only to the very rudiments of the masonic science." (Symbolism of Freemasonry, p. 310.)There are many to-day who are not satisfied with these preliminary acquirements, and the cry for "More Light" is being heard in every quarter of the Masonic world. Intelligent Masons are beginning to realize that there is something more in our symbols and legends, and they are seeking their inner and ultimate meaning.

Let us aid in this work by making our Lodges schools, our labour study, our wages learning, thus may we attain that knowledge of